"There is no substitute for a rigorous and thorough qualitative research, if one wishes to gain deep and nuanced understanding of school cultural ethos in contemporary heterogeneous societies, aiming at forging core curriculum. Markovich's book grapples with this task most impressively. Viewing the school as one of the major sites in which national identities are iterated and reiterated, inculcated and contested, in nationally, racially, ethnically and culturally diverse societies, her book is sure to become a significant contribution not only to the study of the Israeli education system but also to the study of education systems worldwide featuring similar background conditions."
—*Yossi Yonah, Ben-Gurion University of the Negev, Israel*

Nationality and Ethnicity in an Israeli School

Nationality and Ethnicity in an Israeli School: A Case Study of Jewish-Arab Students explores the intersection of ethnicity, nationality, and social structure which is experienced through schooling and its effects on the performance of disadvantaged students.

The book sheds light on the ramifications of the multilayered ethnic-class identities and explores the role of nationality in the reproduction of a depoliticised ethnic hierarchy in school and society. It offers an ethnographic case study of one Israeli high school that adopted critical pedagogy in order to empower underprivileged students that belonged to second and third generation of immigrant Jews from Arab countries. It also analyses the ways in which educational gaps are reproduced through the dominant national culture and identity and discusses the educational consequences of multiethnic school settings.

The book will appeal to students, researchers, and academics in the fields of sociology of education, education policy, peace education, Israeli studies, and critical pedagogy studies.

Dalya Yafa Markovich is a senior lecturer of Education and Sociology in Beit Berl College, Israel.

Routledge Research in Educational Equality and Diversity

Nationality and Ethnicity in an Israeli School
A Case Study of Jewish-Arab Students

Dalya Yafa Markovich

Routledge
Taylor & Francis Group

LONDON AND NEW YORK

First published 2020
by Routledge
2 Park Square, Milton Park, Abingdon, Oxon, OX14 4RN

and by Routledge
52 Vanderbilt Avenue, New York, NY 10017

*Routledge is an imprint of the Taylor & Francis Group, an informa
business*

First issued in paperback 2021

British Library Cataloguing-in-Publication Data
A catalogue record for this book is available from the British
Library

Library of Congress Cataloging-in-Publication Data
A catalog record has been requested for this book

ISBN: 978-1-138-61302-7 (hbk)
ISBN: 978-1-03-209069-6 (pbk)
ISBN: 978-0-429-46483-6 (ebk)

Typeset in Times New Roman
by codeMantra

Contents

Acknowledgments

I want to thank Mandel Leadership Institute, Israel and Beit Berl College that made this book possible.

1 Introduction

The intersection between ethnicity and class and its implications for the academic achievements of students from underprivileged ethnic groups is challenging the educational systems in the West. Special attention has been given to the case of multiethnic societies, such as the U.S., Canada, and Australia. In recent years, this tendency has also been raising concern in nation states in Asia. A vast body of research has been dedicated to the effects of marginalised ethnic-class identity/culture on students' achievements, performance, attitudes, and self-esteem. But ethnicity and class alone cannot tell the whole story of the complex challenges that the ethnic-class identity/culture is facing in the modern nation state and its implications for students' performance in everyday life.

My personal biography, especially my high school years, which took place in a huge, neglected, and violent vocational school, in a small developmental town in the periphery of Israel, led me to investigate the complex ties between ethnicity and class and underprivileged students' performance in school. I was mainly interested in the effect that school has on the perceptions and motivations of students, and in the ways that the school's ideology and pedagogy are tackling the students' ethnic-class underprivilegedness. This line of inquiry is usually adopted when critical pedagogy and underprivileged students are at stake (see, among others, hooks, 1994; Banks & McGee Banks, 2010; Giroux, 2011). With this approach in mind I started a long-term study in *Kedma*, a small school that was established in one of the low-income Jewish neighborhoods in Jerusalem and serves students of Middle Eastern and North African origin (*Mizrahim*). The *Kedma* school has an exceptional biography. The school was one of the first in Israel to be founded by students, activists, and parents who integrated the principles of critical pedagogy, in order to empower the students' marginal ethnic-class position/identity and improve their scholastic achievements. In so doing, they unraveled the cultural lines that define the

Israeli nationality, while reconnecting to the Arab heritage and cultural traditions of the *Mizrahi* Jews that were expelled from the Zionist culture/identity. Thus, as I delved into the school's everyday life, while trying to unveil the relationships between ethnicity, class, and learning *vis-à-vis* critical pedagogy, the tension between ethnicity, class, and other social variables, especially nationality, began to surface. Nationality is almost absent from the research dedicated to underprivileged students that share with privileged students the same national group. As a characteristic that is not considered as a "divider," nationality is usually taken for granted and treated as a transparent variable. In case studies where nationality is perceived as a social unifier, like in relatively young nation states, nationality is even less visible in studies dedicated to learning obstacles and failure. But what happens when the nation is constructed of groups that share the same beliefs regarding their primordial ancestors and collective future, and at the same time comprise different ethnic origins and cultures? How does the national education system and discourse deal with varying degrees of ethnic and cultural heterogeneity, and how does the national educational discourse affect underprivileged ethnic-class groups? The years I spent in *Kedma* exposed the constant clash between the communities' culture and the national dominant culture, as it was presented by the education system. These clashes poked out from the formal textbooks, rituals, ceremonies, and extracurricular programs that were presented in school. Soon these educational sites became mini battlefields in which the dominant national culture was constantly analysed, negotiated, and even hacked by students, and sometimes by teachers and parents as well. Thus, the different ways in which the school's culture was written against the background of the national façade were emerging as the research's focal point. The diverse variety of narratives and practices that were contested, translated, and reshaped by the school exposed the national culture as the main ideological issue that divided the underprivileged students from the formal learning environment and experience. The various ways in which the students, teachers, and parents handled this division, which was manifested through various sites, discussions, and events, tell the story played by nationality in national education systems in multiethnic societies, and explore the role of nationality in the reproduction of a depoliticised ethnic hierarchy in school. By outlining the processes that construct the marginality "from within" the national boundaries of groups that do not challenge their national belonging and republican obligations, the *Kedma* case study sheds light on the ramifications of the multilayered ethnic-class identity for national schooling in Israel and beyond.

2   Analytical fields

In its "ideal" form, the nation's identity and culture is congruent with that of the ethnic origins that constitute the nation state. In other words, the nation state is considered as a natural proceeding of a pre-modern ethnie; the pre-modern ethnie is perceived as transforming itself into the modern nation state (Kohn, 1944). From this point of view, the nation state relies on a primordial attachment that includes common language, myths, symbols, rituals, and blood. These characteristics, which are supposed to be rooted in the groups' ethnic descent, define the modern nation state as a mixture of biology and cultural patterns. Hence, the moment in political history where ethnicity and nationality intersected and constructed a new social category, a new "we," a new kind of solidarity, is when the ethnic sentiments were considered to be overlapping the national political ideology (van den Berghe, 1978). This "organic nationalism," which is based on kinship ties (Pearson, 1988), blurs any attempt at becoming mixed, hybrid, or hyphened. From this point of view, ethnicity and nationality become one, while mismatches, ambivalence, and deviations are not considered as possible options. In other words, ethnicity is perceived as a fixed and stable social phenomenon that develops in and of itself. This argument not only understands nationality as a new phase of ethnicity, but also stresses that ethnicity is an extension of some kind of evolutionary natural development. In light of these assumptions, sharp boundaries have been drawn between the "true" characteristics of the nation – those of the hegemonic ethnic group – and other ethnic group(s) that do not intersect with the nation state but still find themselves part of the nation state. During the process that ends in the birth of the nation, the ethnic groups that do not merge into the national culture and identity are positioned in a rather marginalised social category – that of the "Other." Being labeled as essentially different, the "Other" can suffer from ethnocentrism combined with various ethno-biological separatist myths, which in some political constellations can lead to the worst forms of racism and xenophobia. It is important to note that even though this approach has gained a lot of force, it cannot explain nationalities that are not based on one central ethnicity but on a more voluntary-civic foundation (Greenfeld, 1992). Furthermore, this approach draws sharp lines between the hegemonic ethnic-national group and the other ethnic groups that live in the nation state but did not merged "naturally" into the national culture/identity. While the "Others" are considered as parts of the society, the positioning of their otherness on essential grounds prevents them from imagining themselves as part of the nation. From this point of view, the "Otherness" can barely be rescued from its marginal social position, since the revival of the nation is not considered as a contingent or a non-deterministic phenomenon. Thus, the distinction between the groups is neither perceived as temporary nor understood as the product of a collective cultural work that is constructed in light of power relations and interests. When the main definer of the nation's existence is an atavistic passion combined with natural-biological forces, the "Other" ethnic-class groups have to constantly fight over their social place and position.

The critical thinking adopted in this study lingers on the ways ethnicity is structured within the nation state, emphasising the different roles that ethnicity takes in the process of nation building, and the interests and aims that ethnicity is forced to serve within the national discourse (Balibar and Wallerstein, 1991). From this point of view, the "natural" ethnic roots of the nation reflect the social power, political interests, and economic changes affecting the nation (Gellner, 1964). Thus, the national culture is not just a simple reflection of the ethnic origin of its inhabitants, but also a product of complex social changes. Hobsbawm (1983) described it as an intense cultural work which he called an "invented tradition," while Anderson (2006) emphasised the role of the discursive practices in establishing the cultural platform of the nation. Either way, the social construction of the dominant national culture is perceived as reflecting the interests of the group that wishes to seize control. Even though the "imagination" process is understood by some scholars as part of a variety of a priori ethnic factors (Smith, 2009), it is agreed that these symbolic resources – or in Smith's words "ethno-symbolists" – play a major role in forming the national collective and implementing national belonging. Thus, the "thing" that ties the members of the nation together is described as a network of mutual cultural relations. The somewhat cacophonous combination of the myths of the ancestry, the collective cultural markers, and the shared memories, together with economic, social, and political forces, determines the core of the nation's culture as:

> A named and self-defining human community whose members cultivate shared memories, symbols, myths, traditions and values, inhabit and are attached to historic territories or "homelands", create and disseminate a distinctive public culture, and observe shared customs and standardized laws.
>
> (Smith, 2009, p. 29)

This definition of the nation overlaps with the definition of ethnicity, thus hinting at the complex interplay between the nation and the ethnie, and at the central role and impact of the ethnic culture on the process of nation formation (Smith, 1986). But ethnicity and nationality are two constructed entities that do not necessarily intersect. In other words, the juncture between pre-existing cultural ties and nationality includes complicated interactions between the two. Different ethnic/religious groups from different class positions may support different cultural narratives of the nation. This fragmentation of the "authentic" character and image of the nation can provide antagonistic cultural models and lead to ethnic confrontations over the "real" tradition and heritage of the nation. The ethnos that may take control over the nationalisation project and become dominant in it will be the ethnos that has more political power, as in the case of the culture of the English people that became hegemonic in Britain. A different kind of ethnos may be eroded in this process and lose its status, as in the case of the Welsh people. In cases like this, the incorporation of ethnicity and nationality becomes a violent process related to social control. The ethnic markers that will be identified with the ideal/imagined national culture will gain social, cultural, and political capital in the nation-to-be, due to their role in the nation-building project that will enable them to transform themselves from particular markers to dominant markers (Hall, 2000). The ethnic markers that will not fulfill the same role in the national homogenisation process will issue the lowest rungs of the stratified social structure. From this point of view, ethnicity and nationality do not form a harmonious entity that is restrained by biological features. This is not to say that ethnic and national ties are purely abstract entities. While nationality may blur distinct identities and unite them together in one common cultural alliance (transforming and recreating the "Other from within" as "one of us"), it can also sharply delineate identities and differences between groups that were not distinct prior to its appearance, as a counter-reaction to the national dominance (Rabinowitz, 2001). Thus, the cultural solidarity of the nation and the continuity of the forms and features that underpin the nation's cultural base are a matter of constant negotiation and conflict.

Mass education is one of the channels that has played a crucial role in national socialisation (Gellner, 1983). Even though educational institutions are not the only agencies through which the culture of the nation is transmitted, the modern education system is seen as a vehicle that crafts the cultural forms of the nation. Thus, the modern education system is a platform that serves homogenisation and unification processes. The unifying function of school is carried out by using language, myths, rituals, and symbols that strive to create a cultural cohesion that secures the nation's roots (Weber, 2003). This process of cultural uniformity is achieved through policies and programs that implement the national vocabulary in the narrative, language, curriculum, and institutional practices that are being used in schools. Competing discourses that aim to sabotage the national culture are silenced. Even though the nation is forged out of diverse sub-cultures and different ethnic groups, the education system usually works to neutralise their impact on schools/students.

As shaping and being shaped by the cultural-ideological foundations of the nation, the education system is controlled by the state. In most of the Western nations, the state has the monopoly on the education system's regulations and quality (even when parts of the system are not state-sponsored). The state's monopoly confirms that the manufacturing and transmitting process of the dominant culture will work efficiently. In other words, the state's supervision is essential for constructing identification with the national identity and integrating the new generation of students under one national umbrella. Thus, the process of diffusion is produced and reproduced by various mechanisms of control that guard the borders of the national culture and try to eradicate any cultural discourse that challenges the dominant political structure (Westheimer, 2007). The different routes that the national culture formation process takes in schools are not disconnected from the social-ideological forces that strive to preserve, or change, the national culture.

The impact of education on processes of nationalisation is discussed extensively in the literature, especially when the education system reflects the dominant national culture. The fundamental bond between national culture and education has been analysed mainly through the effect of school on learners from different origin groups. A vast body of studies assumes that background variables may predict the achievements of students from non-hegemonic ethnic-cultural groups in correspondence with the extent of school integration. A negative relationship was found between educational attainment and ethnicity when the students' ethnic identity/culture was marginalised (Tomlinson, 1982; Portes and MacLeod, 1996; Fergus, 2009). Educational attainment in the national education system was also associated with ethnic-cultural stratification (Ogbu, 1990; Mickelson, 2001; Lucas and Berends, 2002; Carter, 2003; Muller et al., 2010), and with an ethnic-cultural limited sphere of participation in the economic field [SES] (Ramey and Suarez, 1985; Entwisle et al., 1997; Gamoran, 2001; Downey et al., 2004). Students from ethnic-cultural minorities who attend the national education system are assumed to perform not only poor academic achievements, but also low self-esteem, and low expectations from the educational process. Findings have shown that aspirations of students vary according to the social position of their ethnic-cultural origin in the nation state (Hanson, 1994; Rigsby, Stull and Morse-Kelley, 1997; Carter, 1999; Khattab, 2015). Therefore, students from ethnic-cultural minorities have had lower aspirations due to the stereotypes and prejudice that were ascribed to them by the dominant national culture (Ogbu, 1978, 1991; Farrell et al., 1994; Kao and Tienda, 1995; Steele, Spencer and Aronson, 2002). As Hannum and Buchman (2003) noted, "it is not safe to assume that expansion in access to education will allow disadvantaged minorities to 'catch up' with initially advantaged ethnic groups, at least in the short run" (p. 510). School integration thus affected the measure of inter-ethnic (in)tolerance. Being exposed to the cultural knowledge of the "Other" ethnic group is correlated with a positive attitude toward that group and with better educational attainment of students from the marginalised culture. In nation states that are characterised by ethnic exclusionism, and in democracies that have been recently established, the in-group favoritism and the out-group hostility increase and affect the educational attainment of the excluded ethnic-cultural groups (Coenders and Scheepers, 2003).

The Israeli case study reflects a state that seeks to unite diverse ethnic-Jewish groups in a single national culture/identity. This mission was carried out by Zionist Jewish pioneers in *Palestine/Eretz Israel* since the days of the *Yishuv* (in Hebrew – settlement – refers to the pre-state Jewish community in *Palestine/Eretz Israel*). The culture constructed by the first settlers was presented as the national narrative; the national narrative was interpreted through the cultural features of the first settlers. This national culture relied on the narratives and cultural traditions that were imported from Europe, since most pioneers migrated from Eastern and Central European countries/regions (*Ashkenazim*). Hence, the pioneers' sources of inspiration, while developing the Zionist local culture, were not connected to middle-Eastern cultures or traditions. Moreover, this evolving national culture did not affirm any historical, geographical, or cultural connection to the Arab world surrounding it. Thus, while the *Ashkenazi* Zionist settlers were geographically returning to the East, they were striving to ideologically return to the West – constructing a *Yishuv* that relied on socialist, secular, and modern notions (Piterberg, 1996). It is important to note that the *Ashkenazi* Zionist settlers' connection to East-European Jewish culture was also characterised by a great ambivalence. On the one hand, Jewishness (as both culture and religion) was the common denominator of the new nation state they wished to build, and thus they strived to gather Jews from all parts of the world to *Palestine/ Eretz Yisrael*. On the other hand, as a secular movement, the *Ashkenazi* Zionist settlers wished to "negate exile" – to reject the Jewish diasporic culture that relied heavily on the Jewish tradition as the only way of life (Raz-Krakotzkin, 2013). In other words, the *Ashkenazi* pioneers' imagined national culture wished to construct a sovereign Zionist state in the Middle East and to connect the Jews, all Jews, with a modernist Western culture that was invented "ex nihilo." The arrival of the massive migration waves of Jewish communities from Arab and Muslim countries (*Mizrahim*) to Israel in the 1950s and 1960s disrupted the *Ashkenazi* pioneers' national-cultural imagined community, causing a "cultural chaos." The *Mizrahi* migrants were perceived as "primitive" and "degenerate," and even identified as having a "retarded mentality" and "battered inelegance" (Frankenstein, 1951, 1952, 1972a, 1972b). These claims posited the *Mizrahi* group's inferiority as almost biological, due to the physical and mental conditions that characterised the Muslim/Arab countries in which they had been socialised for generations. These mental and cognitive "stagnation" marked the *Mizrahim* with the term *eda* or *edot Hamizrach* (sect, or communities of *Mizrahim*). This term served to divide the *Mizrahim* as a whole from the *Ashkenazi* Zionist dominant group, based on their different origin and culture. This symbolic boundary did not serve as a political division (as in the case of the Palestinian communities that remained in Israel after '48), but rather as a cultural division that pointed to the gap between the two ethnic collectives. Furthermore, the term *eda* lumped together a mixed group of migrants from different social, economic, cultural, and linguistic backgrounds, who arrived in Israel from various continents, countries, and regions, including: Babel (Iraq), Iran, Yemen, Syria, Lebanon, Egypt, and north Africa. The term *eda* was forced upon these various groups despite the fundamental differences between them, and thus flattened the various identities, histories, and traditions into one monolithic and labeled social category. This generalising definition was born out of the *Ashkenazi* pioneers' orientalist perspective as well as their ignorance (Khazzoom, 2003). Even though the *eda* was perceived as an un-political term, *edot Ha'mizrach* raised concern and even fear among the Zionist pioneers due to the similarities between the *Mizrahi* migrants' names, culture, music, languages, and traditions and those of the Arabs. The Arabs were perceived as a threat, both to the evolving Jewish nation and to the Westernisation project embedded in it (Shenhav, 2006). The emerging bloody conflict between Jews and Arabs infused the split between *Mizrahim* and *Ashkenazim* and thus increased the potential risks ascribed to the "Arab-Jews," who were forced to de-Arabicise themselves by erasing anything connected to Arabness (Shohat, 1999). Thus, while the *Ashkenazi* Jews, who had immigrated from the diaspora to the "promised land," transformed themselves from the stereotypical anti-Semitic, Orientalised, and feminised framings into the Euro-American model of the pioneer, they identified the Jewish migrants from the Arab-Muslim world with those same orientalist images (Boyarin, 1997). In this context, the pioneers' culture was recognised as the desired cultural model, while *edot Ha'mizrach* were situated against this background as culturally inferior. The cultural definition of the nation-state has not only failed to end the conflict between the various Jewish ethnic groups, but even contributed to the exacerbation of the conflicts. After the state of Israel gained its independence, *edot Ha'mizrach* were caught between two opposing aspirations. On the one hand, *Ashkenazi* Zionist pioneers desired to include *edot Ha'mizrach* in the Israeli nation on the basis of their shared Jewishness. This notion was part of the "ingathering of exiles" – a central layer of the nation building project that imagined all Jews as an inherent part of the Jewish-Israeli nation. On the other hand, *Ashkenazi* Zionist settlers excluded *edot Ha'mizrach* from the Israeli nationality on the basis of their Arab culture (Forum, 2002; Khazzoom, 2008). The inclusion-exclusion paradox reflected the difficulty of eradicating, or at least controlling, the Arab segments of the *Mizrachi* culture. This continuous tension positioned *edot Ha'mizrach* in contrast to the nation, and at the same time as a "natural" part of the nation. The hyphenated position produced *edot Ha'mizrach* as the "Other from within," or in a "neither here nor there" position. This social category constantly collided with the Zionist cultural consciousness. Being located "in between" constituted a marginal social and cultural position that resulted in ethnic divisions in the job market (Semyonov and Lewin-Epstein, 2004), earning capacity (Haberfeld and Cohen, 2007), housing (Bernstein and Swirski, 1982), geographical location (Yifatchel, 1998), political representation (Herzog, 1987), academic achievements (Ayalon and Shavit, 2004), and attainment of higher education (Addi-Raccah and Ayalon, 2008). This social inequality (Yaish, 2001), including *Mizrahi-Ashkenazi* educational gaps in the third generation (Cohen, Lewin-Epstein and Lazarus, 2019), continues to this day. The ethnic stratification has even strengthened the nationalist outlook and the process of de-Arabisation, emphasising simultaneously the binary distinction between Arabs and Jews, while regrading even to non-Jewish growing populations mainly as non-Arabs (Lustick, 1999), and blurring all similarities between Arabs and (*Mizrahi*) Jews. The geo-cultural dialectical synthesis between the Arab and Jewish Middle-Eastern cultures, which was about to create a third *Levantine* space that would promote an alternative pluralistic-integrative co-existence (Kahanoff, 1958; Alkalay, 1993; Ohana, 2011), was de-legitimised by the all-embracing Zionist national approach. In this political process of national-collective identity formation, *Mizrahim* used various practices in order to hide and even deny expressions of their "Arabness" (Chetrit, 1999). Thus, while doing that, they were further strengthening the ethnic structure of the Israeli society and the racist assumptions underpinning it (Yonah, Ram and Markovich, 2010). Opponents of this process were accused of being passive migrants who lacked the needed agency in order to assimilate in the Israeli society, and thus stuck in a whining mentality that promotes an unjustified victimisation discourse. This victimisation discourse was constructed in the Israeli society as not legit, since other members of society were considered as not less victims than the *Mizarhim*, and since being a victim was considered as not willing to sacrifice (Shemer, 2007). Those who tried to "pass" as Israelis (i.e., gain *Ashkenazi* habitus while labeling themselves as "non-ethnic") were often labeled with denigrating nicknames such as "*Mishtaknez*" (in Hebrew – becoming an *Ashkenazi*) or "Shehordini" (in Hebrew – an unsuccessful blend of black and blond) (Sasson-Levi and Shoshana, 2013).

The efforts (and lack of efforts) to internalise the hegemonic national discourse/culture, and their partial failure, laid the foundations for the invention of a new *Mizrahi* culture/identity by second- and third-generation *Mizrahi* immigrants. The new culture/identity was delineated along the contours of the "authentic" *Mizrahi* culture, as well as on a new reinterpretation of their Arab background. This cultural rehabilitation served as an act of protest against the silencing of the *Mizrahi* voices, histories, and traditions. Reinventing the *Mizrahi* identity/culture as a mixed Jewish-Arab affiliation served as a strategy that exposed the *Mizrahim's* double consciousness, positioning, and habitus in the Israeli society – being united nationally and divided ethnically (Shenhav and Hever, 2012). Furthermore, the Arab Jewish possibility proposed a radical, new, political reconstruction of the Zionist narrative, which crossed the national boundaries put up by the *Ashkenazi*-Zionist cultural model. This move wished to create a national hybrid, an oxymoronic category, which not only rejected the Zionist binary offer, but also rejected the fixed ethnic-national homogeneous categories that were forced on both Jewish and Arab identities (Chetrit, 2010). Equipped with N.G.O's, periodicals, and a radical discourse (Kozłowska, 2014), the critical activists grew into a cultural movement that strived to "Levantinise" the Israeli Jewish society (Yonah, Na'aman and Machlev, 2007). One of their main accomplishments was the founding of the *Kedma School* network. Thus, the Arab Jewish identity/culture's problematisation of the standardised ethnic-national categories aroused tremendous criticism and accelerated a heated public debate, even though a binational Jewish-Arab state already existed within the current borders of Israel due to its Jewish-Palestinian composition. The Arab Jews were blamed for emphasising false ethnic markers/images that were no longer valid in the Jewish-Israeli society, thus trying to prove a false identity, and even to "pass" as Arabs, in order to jeopardise the national solidarity (Chetrit, 2010). Moreover, their claims were looked upon as dividing, and even as representing racism toward Jewish Zionism (Dahan and Levy, 2000). Yet despite the fact that the Arab Jewish identity/culture exposed the pitfalls of the Zionist cultural "melting pot," *Mizrahim* and *Ashkenazim* were still united under the powerful national ideological umbrella – that of Zionism. Objecting to this unification was perceived as "releasing the ethnic genie from the bottle" (Levy, 2017). The ability to socialise *Mizrahi* students into the national culture, the cultural work invested in this project, and the different ways national identity/culture reinforce power relations along ethnic-class lines are at the heart of this book's journey along the education system's ideological borders.

3   The field – the *Kedma* School

The *Kedma School*, whose name means "East" in Hebrew, was one of the products of the Arab Jewish movement founded by *Mizrahi* intellectuals and activists. The movement strived to change the face of the Israeli education system by developing 15 high-quality schools in underprivileged areas throughout Israel. The Jerusalem branch, together with the residents of the *Gonenim* neighborhood, established the *Kedma Jerusalem* high school. *Gonenim* – as the area was named in Hebrew – is still called by the neighborhood's residents *Katamonim*, after its former Palestinian name. *Gonenim/Katamonim* is located in the southwest part of the city. In 1952, a massive housing project was built in the area in order to accommodate the Jewish *Olim* ("going up" in Hebrew) who immigrated from Arab and Muslim countries. Most of the neighborhood's tenements were built quickly, using cheap building materials like prefabricated concrete. The buildings included small apartment blocks (sizes range between 25 and 65 square meters) that were partly owned by the government. The small apartments were populated with large families, transforming the neighborhood into one of the most crowded in the city and creating an "internal frontier" region comprised mostly of ethnic minorities. Aharon Dolev, a reporter for one of the biggest newspapers in Israel at that time, described the crowded blocks as "A busy beehive that resembles the inferno [...] A cancerous growth that is identified with countries that have a destructive housing policy that perpetuates distressed slums." (1976, p. 77) During the '70s, a large national rehabilitation project was conducted in the neighborhood. The project's managers invested mainly in renovating the old rundown buildings' facades and in the development of public play grounds, but barley invested in the social and cultural needs of the community (Menachem, 1983). On top of that, over the years, the *Katamonim* neighborhood was known as one of the poorest and most neglected Jewish areas in Jerusalem and as a hotbed of crime (Yona, 2002). The term "the *Katamonim* curse" was usually attached to the neighborhood by the press, thus further demarcating the *Mizrahim* as stigmatised "Others" populating the margins of the Zionist space/narrative. Besides the poverty and neglect, the area lacked essential public services, like a family health center, a community center, and public playgrounds. The neighborhood also lacked high standard educational services. The only school that operated in the neighborhood was a grammar public school, which was classified as one of the poorest achievers in the city. The school was accused of having mostly non-professional staff, consisting of inexperienced teacher trainees. The staff was also accused of stigmatising the students and thus impairing their attitude and motivation for learning (Kedma, 1999). After 6th grade, the students had to attend a comprehensive high-school, named *Denemark*, which is located in a more prestigious neighborhood. During their studies at *Denemark*, a lot of students were subjected to discriminatory treatment and were directed to low-prestige semi-professional learning tracks (Yona, 2002). Other students were enrolled in high schools that were in different locations in the city and offered low standards of learning. Most of the students from the neighborhood did not manage to study in the matriculation tracks and did not attend the matriculation exams. On average, only 10% of the 12th graders from the neighborhood achieved full matriculation certificate (Kedma, 2001), while the national rate of full matriculation certificate at that time stood at 41.4% (Swirski and Atkin, 2002). Today, in addition to the *Mizrahi* residents, the neighborhood is also home to underprivileged Jewish immigrants from the Eastern republics of the former Soviet Union and from Ethiopia, and is still suffering from low academic achievements. The *Kedma* School began to operate in this atmosphere and became the first secular academic (non-vocational) high school in the neighborhood. The main founders of the *Kedma* School grew up in the *Katamonim*, and thus wished to locate the school in the neighborhood. Most of them were at that time students at the Hebrew University of Jerusalem. None of them had any experience in teaching, except for the group's organiser – Clara Yona-Meshumar – who worked and managed various extracurricular learning projects and would go on to serve as the school's first principal (Menashe, 2015). The group was accompanied by Dr. Shlomo Svirsky, one of the founders of the "*Hila* Association for Education in neighborhoods and development towns," which supports parents with the aim of integrating them into the pedagogical process as significant and influential participants, and assists parents with legal aid in order to improve the quality of their children's education. Clara remembers that period as the most intense time of her life:

> We were working around the clock. Setting up meetings with people from the municipality, with the neighborhood's residents, with local politicians. We didn't have an office or a timetable. Most of us were bachelors, so we had plenty of time without having any private obligations. Building the school from scratch was the main thing that occupied our time. It occupied us 24/7.

After a long struggle, both legal and financial, the initiators managed to get permission from the minister of education at that time – prof. Amnon Rubinstein – to open a school of their own. The school founders then embarked on a long journey, trying to convince parents from the neighborhood that had a child that completed his/her studies at the local grammar school to join the new educational adventure. Clara describes this process as working against all odds:

> We split into small groups and started going around the neighborhood. Knocking on doors. Asking people to invite us in for coffee [...] We then talked with the parents about education, grouping, discrimination, ethnicity, the issue of the matriculation exams, and about *Kedma*. The parents asked us: "How can I believe you?" Some of them said: "We had people here from so many projects before, why do you think that you will succeed?" We went from house to house, from door to door. When the first group of parents was consolidated, we started working with them so that they would understand the school's concept and principles and be involved in every part of the way.

The *Kedma* School finally started to operate on 1 September 1994, with 43 students who made up two 7th grade classes. As an "evolving school," *Kedma* aimed to reach the 12th grade in the future (Kedma, n.d.). While *Kedma* in Jerusalem opened its doors, the school's association, named "*Hinuch Hadash*" ("New Education" in Hebrew), managed to open a school in *Kiryat Malakhy*, a development town in the southern district of Israel, and in the *Hatikva* neighborhood, one of the poorest quarters in Tel Aviv. *Kedma* in *Kiryat Malakhy* was closed immediately after the beginning of that year because the founders did not get the approval of the Ministry of Education. *Kedma* in Tel Aviv was closed after five years due to harsh disagreements with the local community and the TLV municipality (Markovich, 1999). Even though *Kedma Jerusalem* started to operate officially, the school initiators faced two major problems: the school was still unauthorised by the Jerusalem education division (JED), and thus did not manage to find an appropriate place to conduct the studies. Thus, *Kedma* began to operate in an old bank branch that was rented by the school's association. Clara describes that place as "A deserted building that had turned into a junkies' den." The *Kedma* association had to invest a lot of efforts, time, and money in order to renovate the place and make it qualified for studying. The old bank building was in a distant area of the city, obliging the school's association to fund transportation for the students. A few months later, the school had to move to another location – an abandoned garage in the industrial part of the city – after the residents that lived near the bank claimed that the school was a noise hazard and managed to get an evacuation order from court. Furthermore, the residents understood the ethnic orientation of *Kedma* and the critical pedagogy adopted by the school as a kind of ethno-centrism, claiming that they do not want to offer hospitality to what they called "A school with a racist perception." (Yona, 2002, p. 95) Until the school managed to leave the bank and move to the garage, the students and teachers had to conduct the studies "undercover": "The staff had to cover the windows with black cardboards and be very quiet, so that the residents won't hear us and complain that we were breaking the court's order." By that time, the school's association was suffering from severe funding problems due to the high costs of the renovation, renting fees, and transportation, and was about to declare bankruptcy. As a result, the teachers did not get their salaries for over seven months. But despite all these difficulties, the school managed to conduct studies in the garage until 1995. Only after the students and the teachers declared a strike and sat for a few days in *Safra square* in front of the Town Hall, and only after the police arrested Clara, the school's principal, in front of the students' eyes for encouraging an illegal demonstration, did a new, intense negotiation with the Jerusalem education division begin. After receiving permission to operate from the municipality, *Kedma* moved to a small wooden shed located in the outskirts of the *Katamonim* neighborhood:

> The shed was very crowded. There weren't any corridors. You would get out of the class straight onto the road. There wasn't any yard. It used to be a kindergarten once, so we had a sandpit... In the summer it got really hot and, in the winter, extremely cold. Every time it was raining the roof leaked. And it rains a lot in

Jerusalem. We were studying there – four classes, 85 students. The parents were shocked when they first saw the shed. The garage looked like a great option compared to these conditions. The only thing that encouraged the parents was the municipality's promise that it was temporary. We studied in the shed until 1996.

Only in its third year, and after Benny Begin, a former member of the Knesset (the Israeli parliament), interfered and convinced Ehud Olmert, the mayor of Jerusalem at the time, of the importance of the matter, *Kedma* got its permanent place in the *Katamonim* neighborhood. *Kedma* is located, to this day, in the same building, which used to be part of a vocational high school that served underprivileged orthodox students from the neighborhood. Even though the facility is not equipped with a laboratory, sports field, or auditorium, the school's community was very glad to move to its current location. The place – an old two-story building covered with small red bricks – is constructed in the shape of a narrow rectangle. A big fenced yard made of asphalt surrounds it. A withered garden full of trash and needles, which has been renovated after years of neglect, is situated between the main road and the school. The school's geometrical structure stands in front of one of the longest and most vastly populated streets that stretch along the length of the neighborhood, packed with concrete blocks. Inside the building, thin walls divide the space into small classrooms. The classrooms are painted white. Each of them has a blackboard and a bunch of tables and chairs made of gray plastic, all bathed in florescent lights. The windows are covered with black grates. The whole structure echoes the modern functional bureaucratic compartmentalisation that characterises most of the school buildings in Israel. This ascetic design, which once relied on the notion of the industrial assembly line, sets *Kedma*, despite its ideological uniqueness, in rather banal visual surroundings. Clara said:

> When we first arrived in this place, we realized that we finally had a place but didn't have a "place." In order to transform this place into our place we had to construct *Kedma* from the inside. To carve our "home" out of that building.

Kedma was covered with the political narrative of its founders, which served as its visual landscape for years. Instead of the national and moral themes that usually decorate schools in Israel, the *Kedma* walls talked in a different ideological language. The school's architectural boredom was covered with large photographs describing different stages of the school's struggles, the neighborhood's poor condition, and critical newspaper articles. One of the walls was turned into an interactive newspaper that was managed by the students. The building's double sides – the inside and the outside – served as a metaphor for *Kedma's* liminal position, as a school that existed both in the municipal sphere/discourse and in the critical sphere/discourse.

The parents, teachers, and founders of the school claimed that *Kedma* would offer the students educational services that did not exist in the neighborhood. From a historical point of view, they were right. *Kedma* offered a multilayered change that criticised and challenged the assumptions of the Israeli education policy for the underprivileged. First, until 1994 there was not even one academic school that prepared students for the matriculation exams in any of the poor neighborhoods and developmental towns throughout Israel. By offering low-income towns and neighborhoods only comprehensive and semi-vocational schools, the Israeli formal national education system (named *"Hinuch Mamlachti"*) was developing an ethnic division between *Ashkenazi* and *Mizrahi* students. Channeling the *Mizrahi* students into pre-vocational training programs assumed that this kind of education suited their needs. This tendency started as early as the '50s. Riger, who was one of the vocational training experts at that time, even claimed that the *Mizrahi* students were "Unable to appreciate abstract learning," (1945, p. 47) and thus had to be enrolled in practical studies. Driven by this policy, a vast percentage of *Mizrahi* students were also assigned to special education (Bashi, 1983). Only those students who were recognised as talented were transferred to academic boarding schools (Smilansky and Nevo, 1979), under the assumption that their parents, who were considered as the "desert generation," couldn't contribute to their children's upbringing and socialisation. Today, some of the vocational tracks/schools aim to prepare the students for the matriculation exams, but most of them do not intend to teach for the exams or fail to do so (Haberfeld and Cohen, 1995). Thus, this policy is blamed for playing a crucial role in the creation of Israel's ethnic-working class, as well as in the reinforcement of an ethnic-based division of labor (Saporta and Yonah, 2004). The ethnic separation in the formal education system had further evolved over the years. Even though the neighborhood had grown tremendously since its establishment in the '50s, the semi-vocational system was still setting the tone in the *Katamonim*, sometimes providing the only available school for students in the neighborhood. Second, the founders of *Kedma* also claimed that none of the existing schools offered to the neighborhood's students was adapted to a multicultural curriculum that emphasised the community's *Mizrahi* ethnic origin. Since Israel is still trapped in the process of nation-building in light of the ideological umbrella of the "melting pot" ideology, and since schooling has become the main tool for fostering national socialisation, only limited multicultural practices are implemented in the Israeli schools (Bekerman, 2009), and only a few schools have adopted a multilingual policy (Amara et al., 2009). Hence, mono-culturalism and cultural segregation have become the norm (Dahan and Levy, 2000), while the offered curriculum has reflected the Zionist pioneers' values (Podeh, 2000). Thus, controversial political issues and critical reflections are encouraged only in special and exceptional projects (Rohde, 2012). Furthermore, even though the educational policy emphasises the integration of global and international issues, curriculums have become more Jewish and nationally oriented (Yemini, Bar-Nissan and Shavit, 2014). Without any attention to the Jewish ethnic conflict and the students' cultural background, it was claimed that the *Mizrahi* students from the *Katamonim* did not have good chances to change their attitude toward schooling and raise their motivation to further invest in their studies (Kedma, undated). In order to expand the school's curriculum, the *Kedma* initiators decided to adopt pedagogical ideas, practices, and narratives that were inspired by critical pedagogy (Freire, 1970; Freire and Shor, 1987). This notion assumed that a successful educational process for underprivileged students relied on a critical deconstruction of their oppressive social reality. The main pedagogical tools that were used were the reflective dialogue and critical thinking. This kind of dialogue intended to unveil the students' underprivilegedness, by exposing the socio-historical conditions under which their marginal position was constructed and reproduced within the nation state. By understanding their "Otherness" as a product of oppression (Shor, 1992; McLaren and Kincheloe, 2007), the school was hoping to instigate processes of empowerment anchored in the students' culture and identity. The teachers believed that the process of empowerment would lead to improved academic achievements and self-image, as well as to the students' ability and motivation to learn and to break through social barriers (Freire, 1992; Darder, Baltodano and Torres, 2002). Traditional schooling comprises the bulk of teaching and learning in the Israeli education system. Innovative and critical modes of learning and thinking remain in the margins (Gallagher, Hipkins and Zohar, 2012). Even school principals do not tend to include in their schools' educational roles critical thinking, and especially pedagogies that strive for social justice (Arar, 2015). Thus, conducting studies in light of critical pedagogy was, and still is, a rare decision, that positioned *Kedma* as one of the only high schools founded in Israel to be based on this discourse and praxis (Yona and Zalmanson Levi, 2004). The schools' unique pedagogy was carried out by developing three special programs that were added to the national curriculum, and combined learning materials that were closer to the students' world and worked to deconstruct the stigmatised *Mizrahi* identity (Resnik, 2006). The schools' unique pedagogy was also carried out by the teachers that served also as mentors. Each class was assigned two mentors who thought the class and conducted mentorship meeting with the whole class and with each student and created a nurturing environment that constructed strong relationships between teachers, students, and parents (Ayalon, 2007). Even though the mentoring process resulted in some cases in teacher burnout, the process contributed to the school's unique pedagogy and political goals (Bairey Ben-Ishay, 1998). Fourth, the school was at that time the only school in Israel that was established by underprivileged parents together with students and activists. To this day, this is a rare phenomenon in the Israeli education system. Most magnet schools in Israel are part of the liberalisation and parental choice trend that started in the '80s, and is led by middle and upper-class, mostly *Ashkenazi* parents. These strong communities could open semi-private schools in light of their unique cultures, pedagogical trends, and fields of interest (Swirski and Dagan-Buzaglo, 2009), while the culture of *Mizrahim* and Palestinians living in Israel was denied by the educational policy (Al-Haj, 1995; Abu-Saad, 2006). Hence, these unique schools were blamed for deepening the privatisation tendency and the differential distribution of educational services (Dahan, 2011). Furthermore, this policy was weakening the role of the state in the field of education – importing free-market mechanisms, cutting educational services, and reducing public funding ("weak state"), and at the same time continuing to dictate the educational goals and national values to the public schools ("strong state") (Yonah, Dahan and Markovich, 2008). This "weak state"/"strong state" duality was expanding the educational gap while emphasising national unity. As a unique player in this field, *Kedma's* concept of *Mizrahi* "cultural competence" (Avissar, 2019), caused an uproar in the Israeli public discourse (Getz, 2003). Harsh condemnation of the school was to be heard from educational administrations, politicians, reporters, and educational experts. On the educational level, *Kedma* was blamed for conducting improper education while "selling" the neighborhoods' parents promises that couldn't be fulfilled. On the political level, it was also claimed that the *Kedma* project would sabotage the nation's cohesion, due to the school's ideological ideas and especially their intention to highlight the ethnic differences of *Mizrahim* and the effect of these differences on equal opportunities for *Mizrahim* (Yona, 2002). On top of all these accusations, *Kedma* was perceived as racist due to its students' composition. Clara recalls this painful period:

> We never said that the school was only for *Mizrahi* students. We just declared that we were going to open a school in the community, in the neighborhood. Most of the children in the neighborhood are from *Mizrahi* origins. So, we decided to put an emphasis on their culture. What's wrong with that? Why can't I learn about my traditions? Did anyone ever claim that the privileged schools that contain 100% *Ashkenazi* students are racist?

Despite the criticism and to this day, *Kedma* is still operating in the neighborhood, and is still one of the only academic high schools in Israel founded by an underprivileged community, offering a full matriculation track for underprivileged students, and adopting critical pedagogy that emphasises the *Mizrahi* culture. Almost two decades after it was founded, and being the only *Kedma* School still operating, the school has managed to help hundreds of students from the neighborhood, from 19 cohorts of 12th graders, to finish their studies successfully, pass the matriculation exams, and continue their studies at universities and colleges.

4 Methodology

I first came to *Kedma* in the fall of 2001, when the teaching staff decided to conduct a study regarding the ideological principles of the school. The outcome of this process was intended to become the school's pedagogical manifesto. I was asked to join the staff, in what they called "the model meetings," and help with the research process. In the beginning we did not have a clear research plan. Only after a while the research procedure was established. The staff would meet every three weeks during two academic years, in the library – the school's biggest room – for a 2- to 4-hour meeting during the late afternoon, after the school day ended. Infused by the notion that qualitative research can serve as a tool for social change (Bar Shalom and Krumer-Nevo, 2007), I begin to record the meetings with the school's video camera and transcribed them. In each of the meetings I brought the staff the transcription of the previous meeting. The transcribed textual materials helped in sharpening various aspects of the discussion, as well as identifying marginal voices and enabling a more reflective gaze on the issues discussed. After the former meeting was summed up by using the transcriptions, the group moved on and explored new topics and ideas. This process located me in a dual status. On the one hand I was helping to conduct an action research, and on the other hand I started to conduct an ethnography of the whole process. As the research developed, I asked the staff's permission to make observations in more meetings as well as in different classes. After I got the school's permission, I started to attend the staff's professional meetings, teachers-parents' meetings, and the management meetings. I also attended literature, history, art, Bible, and civic classes in the 11th and 12th grades for a whole academic year, as well as special lessons and events, such as: the annual school trip, Holocaust Memorial ceremony, the national Memorial Day for the Fallen Soldiers, IDF recruiting program, student council meetings, youth group presentation, and sex education. I conducted a total of 29 observations of the "model meetings," including a two-day workshop that was dedicated to reviewing and summarising the process and was held at a conference center outside of Jerusalem; 11 observations of the "professional meetings;" four observations of teachers-parents' meetings, including a weekend workshop that was dedicated to discussions between the teachers and parents regarding the school's aims and goals and was held in a hotel outside of Jerusalem; and 62 observations in class. The observations were accompanied by a detailed field diary, where I mentioned various occurrences that took place in real time. I ended the ethnography in 2003 and started conducting interviews for a couple of years (2005). I interviewed the founding teachers, all in all 12 interviews that were recorded with the school's video camera. The teachers that were interviewed were teaching various subjects: literature, history, art, theater, English, civic studies, and Bible. Some of them served only as subject-matter teachers, while others were also homeroom teachers. I then interviewed 15 of the school's first graduates that finished their studies at *Kedma*. The graduates that were interviewed were those that were willing to meet me. They composed a heterogeneous group, among them students that finished their study with a matriculation certificate as well as those who did not attend the exams, students that were involved in school life as well as those that were indifferent, and students that started to study in *Kedma* when the school opened its doors as well as those who joined *Kedma* years after it started to operate. All the students' interviews were recorded with the school's video camera, except for two interviews that were recorded with a tape recorder due to the students' requests. I met the students once again in a class reunion that they held in *Kedma* in 2005. Another part of the data included a vast number of articles that were published about the school in the newspapers and later in social media, and four T.V reports that followed the school's activities, as well as unpublished position papers, minutes, surveys made by an independent research institute, and the school yearbooks. Since I finished the interviews, I have been following the school's activities through its vibrant Facebook page, articles, and the annual conferences held at the school each year. I also follow the *Kedma Foundation for the Advancement of Egalitarian Academic Education in Israel*, which publishes programs and educational resources for teachers and a monthly newsletter that is still published to this day (https://kedma-edu.org.il).

My first visit to *Kedma* during school day caused a bit of an excitement in the small school. It was in the middle of the school year, and I was an outsider who was unfamiliar to the school's small community.

The students were used to meeting "foreigners" in certain circum-
stance: reporters, politicians, supervisors from the municipality or the
Ministry of Education, and curious people who wanted to volunteer in
school, so me being there awakened natural curiosity accompanied by
a lot of questions. On top of that, my *Ashkenazi* appearance attracted
attention, and sparked all kinds of guesses regarding my presence
there. I told the students that I was going to research the school's
activities. I was asked by a couple of students: "What exactly are you
going to check?" I did not know what to answer. "Naturally" I was
driven toward questions regarding the unique pedagogy adopted by
Kedma, and the ways *Kedma* was doing it differently than the regular
public schools in the periphery. But, as the research evolved, the intense meetings with the students, staff members, parents, and learning
activities pushed me from the usual issues regarding underprivilegedness and schooling to a different path that was not just about grades
and educational opportunities. This path was about an unexpected
character – nationality and national culture – that was entwined in
every aspect of everyday school life, both connecting and dividing the
students from the educational apparatus.

5   The matriculation exams

The issue of the matriculation studies, matriculation exams, and matriculation certificate ("Bagrut" in Hebrew) has a key role in the Israeli education system and thus was central to *Kedma's* life. The matriculation process serves as an assessing tool that evaluates the students' knowledge in eight different disciplines (for comparison, see the British A-level and the German Abitur). Gaining a matriculation certificate hence enables the student to gain higher education, as well as certain positions in the labor market. Thus, the studies for the matriculation exams have a dramatic influence on the teaching and learning modes:

> It's a measurement tool [...] that everyone's addicted to. We've created a situation in which school principals, who are supposed to be concerned with developing abilities and imparting knowledge to students, are increasingly busy with exams, so much so that they do not have time left for social activities.
>
> (Volansky, In: Dattel, 2018, p. 27)

This tendency has created an exam culture, occasionally causing a national hysteria, which does not exist to this extent in any other Western country, since success rates in the matriculation exams stand at approximately 50% of the 12th graders (Swirski, Konor-Atias and Dagan-Buzaglo, 2016). This data reveals a gap between Jews and Palestinian students and between *Ashkenazim* and *Mizrahim* students. One of the fundamental variables that predict the ethnic gap is the differentiated investment in students in accordance with their origin and class (Dahan et al., 2003).

In light of the importance ascribed to the matriculation exams, the school and the parents wished the students to study for the exams in order to improve the future opportunities open to them (Kedma, 1999). Passing the exams would also prove that the school's pedagogical way was more suitable to the students' needs, and that the students were not less talented than their privileged counterparts. But studying for the matriculation exams also meant adopting the formal curriculum that the school wished to modify according to the principals of critical pedagogy. The school was investing a lot of effort in developing special programs that touched on the students' identity, culture, and life experiences, that were supposed to inspire critical thinking, empower the students, and strengthen the relationship with the community. Thus, in order to implement the principles of critical pedagogy, the teachers had to expand the formal curriculum, and in some cases even abandon the formal curriculum. Integrating these unique programs with the regular official curriculum (including the curriculum of the matriculation exams) caused a clash between the contradicting goals, aspirations, and praxis and provoked a huge debate between the teachers and the parents and between the teachers themselves. These different approaches divided the teachers and the parents into two camps.

Most of the parents supported a pedagogical process that would lead the students to successfully pass the matriculation exams. A vast majority of these parents were born in Israel to immigrants from Muslim and Arab countries who moved to the neighborhood during the '50s. Only a few of them finished high school and have a high school diploma. Some of the parents work in the service industry, while others are unemployed, and others rely on welfare benefits and disability stipends. Their children studying at *Kedma* were, for the most part, the first child in the family to study in an educational track that prepared students for the matriculation exams. These parents refused to continue the critical learning process. Paradoxically, the critical process, which focused mainly on the students' socio-political experiences and positioning, was viewed by the parents as not dealing with the "real world." The "real world" was that of the matriculation exams. Rachel, a mother of a 10th grader, explained:

> We must push for matriculation because, because that's today's social standard. We want our kids to succeed, we want them to advance, and without a matriculation certificate you can't go near a university. The importance of matriculation is matriculation itself; without matriculation there is no future anywhere to advance to.
>
> Markovich (2013a, p. 7)

Yafit, a mother of a 11th grader, added: "I don't know about all the political talk in school [...] we must play by the rules." Rachel and Yafit anchored the matriculation process/certificate in real-life needs.

For them, the socio-political conditions that excluded their children from proper education system until *Kedma* was founded were not real. They were a speculative assumption. The real-life conditions were the rules. Thus, the necessity embedded in the matriculation exams was justified by a tautology ("the importance of the matriculation is matriculation itself").

Other parents emphasised the connection between success in the matriculation exams and the normative pedagogy used in other schools. Moshe, father of a 10th grader, said:

> The matriculation exam is like conquering a fortified target known as 'matriculation'. We cannot, as of yet, forsake this. That's how life is. We have to do it like every other school does […] because if we do it in other ways […] we might not succeed. This will ruin our kids' chances in life.
>
> Markovich (2013a, p. 7)

The future life that the matriculation exams offered the students was more real than the critical deconstruction of the social reality that critical pedagogy offered. Hence, instead of turning into critical thinkers, they wished to adopt the national educational system's state of mind. The normative causality that ties higher education with good opportunities in the job market and better standards of living, especially integrating into the middle-class, was one of the main reasons for studying among under-privileged groups (Freire and Shore, 1987). This determination was justified by some of the teachers. Ana explained: "We want the children to be able to live in a nice place. To go on holidays abroad. To buy nice stuff." As Abraham, one of the fathers, concluded: "From the start we said, 'everyone can' (succeed in the matriculation exams), that's how we'll beat the system, not with revolutions (Markovich, 2013a, p. 8)." Shula, the mother of a 10th grader, said:

> Taking the matriculation exams means collaborating with the system, but our situation is such that we must succeed and cannot afford to have confrontations right now.
>
> Markovich (2013a, p. 8)

In other words, the critical way of studying was perceived as a privilege that the students did not own. This privilege was ascribed to students that belonged to the middle class. They had the time and the money needed to take adventurous learning paths that deviated from the normative path. David, father of a 9th grader, said:

We must succeed in school. We don't have any other chance than to succeed in school. The kids can't fight for their identity right now. Maybe the privileged kids can do that. Their parents can pay for private education after high school ends, so that they don't need school for studying for the matriculation. And I'm saying that with all due respect to protest.

Thus, parents' relation to critical methods remained loose. Limiting the critical praxis was not the outcome of a lack of understanding. The parents valued the critical approach, and even wished they could join a critical learning process. But in order to cope with their ethnic-class exclusion, they were forced to adopt the national educational discourse. Furthermore, even though most parents acknowledged the importance of criticality, they regarded critical pedagogy as a non-normative option for them. Choosing this option meant relinquishing the normative option, and thus further marginalising themselves from the national education system. Parents of students of color have made similar claims regarding progressive educators, arguing that while they allowed the students to express their feelings, they sabotaged their chances to enter the mainstream (Delpit, 1998).

While most of the parents perceived the critical approach as a "Spanner in the wheels," most of the teachers were enthusiastic about the potential benefits that critical pedagogy had in store for the students. As *Mizrachim* that were born and raised in the *Katamonim* and were exposed to the Jewish-Arab discourse while they were students, the teachers were inspired by critical intellectuals and discourse. Especially, they were determined to turn these abstract ideas into real actions that could change the parents' and students' perspectives. Even though the teachers invested a lot of time and energy in order to prepare the students for the matriculation exams, they tended to criticise the exams while emphasising the tools and views of critical pedagogy. For a dominant group of teachers, the matriculation exams were a form of institutional oppression that exemplified and exposed the meritocratic lie. Efi (male), math teacher, described the matriculation learning process's functions and effects:

I'm not a fan of the matriculation exams. When you use these exams, you encourage the pupils to achieve. But some of them will not be successful in that. Some of them will be left behind. If we are to promoting equality, then by using the format of the exams we are also advancing the message that those who don't do it are not the same (as the students who passed the exams).

Efi claimed that the learning processes that the exams imposed on schools were serving as mechanisms of selection and tracking that reflected individualistic competition. In other words, while studying for the matriculation means a successful experience for some students, by the same token it means failure for others. For Efi, losing those who fail to meet the standards set by the hegemonic forces means reproducing the educational systems' effects that *Kedma* wanted to eradicate. Thus, adopting the notion that favors the students who can handle competitive achievement (and neglecting the under-achievers) reflects and supports the values of the capitalist society that *Kedma* wished to deconstruct. Furthermore, since failure in the meritocratic system is perceived as personal, and not as a result of social construction and excluding forces, the students that fail are labeled as outsiders of the capitalistic system – "(they) are not the same."

Other teachers opposed the exams due to the pedagogical process embedded in the years devoted to studying for the exams. Beti (female), the literature teacher, explained:

> To learn for the exams is to repeat and memorize knowledge. For example, in my field [literature], you have to learn all the hegemonic *Ashkenazi* writers and poets, and you don't ask questions about it. You are not supposed to analyze the political concept of this curriculum. You are not supposed to understand what it serves. Just memorize.

Beti connects the pedagogical tools embedded in the learning process for the exams with the socio-political stratification. In her view, by adopting the hegemony's pedagogical practices, *Kedma* is participating in the marginalisation process instead of illuminating and exposing this process.

The matriculation exam's Eurocentrism, as manifested in the exam's curriculum, was also condemned. Moran (female), the History teacher, emphasised the effect of the content:

> The learning materials for the exams are not ours [...] they don't represent our culture. All the things that I teach are detached from the history of the neighborhood and that of *Mizrachim* in general. They are just not connected to our life at all. At all.

From Moran's point of view, the exams are not just embedded in the oppressive system and reflect the oppressive system, but also take an active role in the structural discrimination through the curriculum that characterises the system. Thus, choosing the achievement-based option (matriculation exams) means choosing the hegemonic narrative option. From this point of view, the critical approach served as a bypass of the reproductive educational system and not necessarily as a route to normative educational success. Some of the teachers even claimed that not achieving a matriculation certificate but choosing an alternative-critical way of studying and knowing the world would be the real success. We are not a "Grade factory, and we don't want to become one," one said. One of the teachers even claimed that by imposing the matriculation learning process on the students they become "Our hostages," as opposed to being empowered. Empowering the students and the community vis-à-vis critical learning and thinking was described as the opposite pole of the tendency to adapt to the system.

This heated debate ended by the school choosing not to abandon the critical gaze, but still devote all their efforts to preparing the students for the matriculation exams. Instead of turning to a critical-driven climate, the parents and teachers chose an achievement-driven climate as a path of integration into the structure of opportunity offered by the national education system/ideology. This decision illuminates how worlds of meaning are acquired in light of different ethnic-class positioning. The parents' choices cannot be explained by a lack of adequate knowledge. On the contrary, the parents understood that they lacked the agency of the privileged class. This agency was not shaped, in their view, by their life experiences, since critical pedagogy was trying to recruit their agency by imposing its praxis on them in a rather dogmatic way. The parents' decision/agency was thus a result of their marginal position. It reflected their way to cope with their ethnic-class exclusion. Since the parents understood the ways certain kinds of socialisation and credentials can offer their holders power over others, they decided that choosing the matriculation track will be more effective for their children's future mobility. Being aware of the limitations embedded in the liberating praxis, and especially of the relativity of the liberating praxis, the parents even blamed critical pedagogy for developing new kinds of oppression. By exposing the pitfalls embedded in the universal message of the liberating praxis, they were pointing at the complex bundles of rights and powers that the liberating messages emphasise, and the ways that those to be emancipated are further driven by these messages to the margins. Perceiving the liberating message and praxis as being also embedded in the thick social network of power relations exposed the liberating message's relativity, in contrast to its all-embracing claims.

Thus, the parents were claiming that the path to liberation is not only camouflaging mechanisms of control, but also camouflaging the power of the national educational system and discourse over critical perspectives. The ways the national educational discourse overshadowed the promise of the critical discourse and differentiated between class and cultural locations was further shown in the perspectives adopted by the students.

6 The students

The critical pedagogy employed by the school aimed not only to improve the students' political awareness regarding their social positioning, but also to empower them. Critical pedagogy wishes to empower underprivileged students on both the personal and the political level. On the personal level, the process of empowerment strives to improve the students' attitude toward learning. Underprivileged students tend to internalise low self-esteem, while ascribing the process of learning, as well as better learning abilities, only to the privileged students. Stigmatised background variables of underprivileged groups, especially ethnicity, race, and class, were found to be connected to poor academic achievements due to their bad influence on students' expectations (Hanson, 1994; Carter, 1999) and aspirations (Ogbu, 1991). On the political level it has been claimed that improving the attitude toward the learning process will strongly affect the underprivileged group's social positions and opportunities. For example, deconstructing the personal failure through critical readings of the social conditions and frames in which the group is embedded is supposed to empower the underprivileged group and infuse social change. Thus, a student that suffers from stigmatisation is supposed to gain power through the learning process, which will enable its group members to deal with their marginalised position in society. Hence, the personal-political empowerment is found to be a crucial process that can overcome the effects of ethnic, race, and class labeling on educational performance (Zirkel, 2008). These findings not only connect attitudes toward learning to political awareness, but also claim that attitudes toward learning determine the groups' ability to exercise power.

Most of the students in *Kedma* were trapped between conflicting messages due to their wish to succeed in school and to their social and economic struggles (Grebelsky-Lichtman, Bar Shalom and Bar Shalom, 2015). The teachers invested a lot of efforts in personal empowerment, so that the students would trust themselves and as a result change their community's stigmatised image and life conditions. This process hoped to disrupt the unequal distribution of educational "goods" and privileges, and construct different opportunities for all underprivileged students. The school's empowering efforts turned out to be effective on the level of improving the students' grades. Even though the students arrived in *Kedma* at 7th grade with low self-esteem and resistance to school, when they graduated, they demonstrated high achievements and developed devotion and warm relationships toward the school and toward studying in general (Dahaf, 2000). In light of these results, the examination of the students' self-perception was supposed to produce encouraging results. But despite the critical pedagogy's assumption, the graduates' self-perception revealed ambivalent opinions that fluctuated between two poles, splitting along binary lines.

On the one hand, the students described themselves as "good students." The good student was identified according to the conventional hierarchical school register. From this point of view, goodness was described in light of the meritocratic definitions as based solely on academic achievements and academic success. But on the other hand, the students' ethnic-class identity and social position labeled them as the "Other" of the Israeli society. Sigal, one of the female students that graduated from *Kedma* with a matriculation certificate, explained the way she perceived herself by posing a question regarding the juxtaposition between her learning skills and grades and the way her ethnic identity and her place of residence were labeled:

> We were constantly told that because we are a school from the hood (the *Katamonin* neighborhood), and because the students are Kurds and Moroccans and from other *Mizrahi* origins, that we are dummies [...] I'm a good student, but, [...] we are a school for students from this neighborhood. What is the meaning of that? Are we good or bad?

Being a good student from the meritocratic point of view, and at the same time labeled as underprivileged due to her ethnic origin, caused a confusion that prevented Sigal from relying solely on her grades when asked to describe her self-image. Racist life experiences were dominant in the perception of underprivileged students (see: Shoshana, 2017), and thus colored the description of Sigal's self-image as a student. In other words, being a *Mizrahi*, when describing her self-image as a student, Sigal could not adopt only the acceptable meanings attached to the "good student." Roni, male student, also struggled with the same dilemma:

When I studied at *Kedma* they (students from other high schools)
kept putting me down. And, I kept asking: 'why do you treat me
differently? Why do you think I'm dumb?' But then again, people
in the neighborhood are not like everyone else, right? This is a
special school, especially for us, right?

Markovich (2014, p. 145)

As part of an ethnic-class labeled group, the students' self-perception
was disrupted in yet another way:

I studied at *Kedma* school, but I kept feeling that I'm not one of
those students, you know, one of the good students from the other
schools. Maybe it's because we were always studying about it [...]
we were always occupied with this question of being marginalized
because of the stuff we studied (*Kedma's* critical pedagogy and
curriculum).

Learning about their marginalised social position, in order to
deconstruct this position, was also sabotaging the students' sense of
belonging to the "good students" group. Instead of transforming the
critical deconstruction of their stigmatised identity into a source of
power (i.e., "black is beautiful"), the school's emphasis on the students'
identity turned their socially constructed identity into an essential
identity. Not "strategic essentialism," but simply essentialism. In other
words, the critical process was constantly reminding the students of
their marginalised position, which kept undermining their self-worth.
Thus, even when the students took part in a critical process that
reflected the mechanism that constructed their marginalisation, the
ethnic stigmatisation was stronger than the process of deconstructing
these labels and raising their educational achievements. In another example, the clash between the students' stigmatised attributes and their
labeled ethnic-class identity was reflected to them by outsiders. This
experience made the students insecure about their status and their
abilities; hence it underestimated their educational achievements.
Yossi, male student, gave an example of this when telling the inter-
viewer about an encounter he had had with students from a privileged
group/school:

I was once dating an *Ashkenazi* girl. She was living in another
neighborhood and studying in a different school [...] I met her
friends once [...] in the beginning I was hiding my origin. She
didn't know that I'm a Moroccan, but, when... but when her
friends heard that I'm from *Kedma*, they, they, it was not important

anymore that I'm studying for the exams just like them. I guess [...]
I mean, we are not like them.

Even though Yossi differentiates between his own personal achievements and his stigmatised identity ("studying for the exams just like
them"), he accepted his inferior structural position, as it was reflected
by his former girlfriend's friends ("we are not like them"). Avi, male
student, also felt that his ethnic characteristics are his most blatant
characteristics:

> Maybe it's true that we can't function in a regular school, I mean in
> a real, regular, academic high school. I mean [...] it's like, if you are
> oppressed for so long you can't do it, you can't just succeed; I mean,
> you can't jump from zero to 100, it doesn't work like that. We were
> on the margins for generations; we studied that in our project ('my
> history') and talked a lot about that with our teachers. When one
> goes through that kind of trauma, one can't just fix it with grades.
>
> Markovich (2014, p. 145)

In this case, Avi anchored the distinction he made between his grades
and his self-worth in the image that was ascribed to the school.
Kedma is perceived as an unregular school because it is in an underprivileged neighborhood. From Avi's point of view, it seems that this
tautology was unbreakable. Furthermore, Avi is aware of the marginalisation the *Mizrahim* went through and of the new consciousness
generated through *Kedma's* learning process, but despite that, Avi's
stigmatised identity is framing his experience in a deterministic way
("[you] can't just fix it with grades"). In other words, when the students
have to "choose" between their achievements and their labeled ethnic
image, they cannot detach their stigmatised ethnic identity from their
self-esteem.

Many other students took this notion to the extreme. These students
did not just define themselves as "Others" but emphasised their "Otherness" to an absurd degree. This "Otherness" took shape against the
background of the vehement criticism that *Kedma* was subjected to
over the years, due to the school's ethnic-class composition and due to
the school's critical approach towards ethnic marginalisation. From
this point of view, the students claimed that they had no other option
but to describe themselves as the "Others" of the school system, or as
"bad students."

The students were exposed to the repetitive and vocal public criticism directed at *Kedma* from day one. Beni, male student, tells about

the ways they were described mostly as *Mizrahim* rather than just students:

> Well... they used to call us... the school for the *Mizrahim*, the school for those disadvantaged, the school that sells illusions to *Mizrahim* that cannot really learn, you understand what I'm saying... like... as if, as if we were some kind of monkeys in a lab, and now the school is doing some kind of a big experiment, maybe a miracle, so... whatever?

Beni adopted a conscious underestimated identity in response to the critics' views. By adopting this identity, he is claiming that because the school and the *Mizrahi* group are being labeled, he was driven to the identity of the "Other." In other words, the identity of the "Other" was forced upon him through his ethnic stigmatisation, preventing him from crossing the meritocratic boundaries even when he was studying in the prestigious matriculation-oriented track. Lili, female student, also articulated her identity by reversing the meritocratic binarism, in response to the harsh public criticisms that were directed at the school:

> I always wanted to show people that (the *Kedma* students) are as good as anyone else. So, I used to try to explain about *Kedma* and, and, tell them that we are as good as the others. I have very good grades. No one gave it to me for free because I'm from Kurd origins... I... I worked very hard to achieve that. But after a while you say... you know what, O.K., we are those bad students from the hood.

Lili wanted to be treated like a regular student, like the "others." But instead, she was viewed as a special student due to her *Mizrahi* (Kurd) origin. Thus, she was forced to articulate her identity in light of the underprivileged perception that was imposed on her. Adi, female student, also claimed that within the hegemonic orientalist narrative she was described first as a stigmatised *Mizrahi*. In her perception, this stereotypical framing overshadowed any other features of herself and her community.

> When they (student from privileged schools) hear that I am from *Kedma* they laugh. Like, like as if we are nothing but people who live in a poor neighborhood. It doesn't matter... so, you know what, we are *arsim*, we are *frehot*. Now deal with this.

Adi was highlighting the *Kedma* students' oriental characteristics against the unmarked hegemonic culture, by using terms that were taken from Arabic and serve in Hebrew for denigration. *Ars* (عَرْص) (*Arsim* in plural) means in Palestinian Arabic a pimp. This term is usually used to describe people from *Mizrahi* origin in order to express their vulgar and violent character. The term *freha* (فرخة) (*Frehot* in plural) means in Moroccan Arabic happiness. This term used to be one of the most common women's first names among Jewish Moroccan emigrants during the '50s. After a while this name was commonly used in the Israeli slang as a pejorative term describing *Mizrahi* women as outlandish, hasty, and tasteless. These terms also appeared in the school yearbook, which was written and produced by the students at the end of their last year in school (12th grade). The majority of the students chose to describe themselves by using the term *ars*. For example: "X is accused of employing about 5,721 innocent girls imported from overseas." Other students used other negative and stereotypical images that are identified with *Mizrahim*, like the thief: "Since being captured for stealing the entire contents of a newsstand, he was disappeared. Last seen in a black Honda next to the refurbishing garage;" "Caught in the south of the country in a cosmetics factory while stealing products worth $1,000;" "Accused of breaking into a factory in Tel Aviv and stealing 7,250 packs of scented toilet paper." Other students described themselves as thugs: "Esther a.k.a 'the nightmare' was caught in a brawl at the Duck Club." And others were described as rapists: "The above is suspected of raping a minor in Acre (Markovich, 2014, p. 146)." Instead of feeling threatened by these images, the students stretched the stereotypes imposed on *Mizrahim* and ridiculed them. Even though this notion accepts the dichotomous meritocratic division – "good student"/"bad student" – in this case the dichotomy was fulfilling a critical role – deliberately increasing the stigmatisation process forced on the students. Research findings have shown that ethnic-class positioning determines the ways underprivileged ethnic-class groups use their ethnicity in order to interpret their inferiority. Most often, *Mizrahim* in Israel tend to deny that they suffer from racism and ethnic marginalisation by denying its existence (Mizrachi and Herzog, 2012). It was found that members of the *Mizrahi* group try to avoid the stigmatisation process in order to emphasise their connection to the national Jewish group. In other words, the voices that challenge the narrative of belonging are dismissed because of the danger they hold. For example, when *Mizrahim* are marginalised by using Arab insulting words like *ars* and *freha*, these labels can blur the distinctions between them and the Arabs and even have the potential of pushing them out of the Jewish collective (Chetrit, 1999). In another example, underprivileged and stigmatised ethnic students did not ascribe their failure in school to ethnic discrimination but to their own choice, in order to avoid the feeling of being shoved out of the collective (Mizrachi, Goodman and Feniger, 2009). Only in rare cases did *Mizrahi* students refuse to de-neutralise ethnicity, even insisting that the school staff paid attention to the ethnic boundaries that mediated their relationships and attitudes toward the school (Tabib-Calif and Lomsky-Feder, 2014). In most cases, by ignoring the stereotypes with which they are labeled, *Mizrahim* tend to counterbalance the Otherisation process directed toward them and prevent a further separation from the national togetherness. The students of *Kedma* did not ignore their ethnic signifiers and the process of labeling they suffered due to these signifiers. Furthermore, the students of *Kedma* did not try to hide their ethnicity and pass as others (for example: as "regular" good students). As opposed to these modes of behavior, the students chose to respond to the labeling they suffered through the years (both labeling processes that were imposed directly on them and those that were imposed on the school) by further labeling themselves as "not good enough students" and as "bad students." This strategy implies that the cultural work needed in order to construct and maintain the imagined national ideal student, or to ignore the ethnic labels, was an option that could not be fulfilled by the students. Thus, their choice – accepting and using the stigmatising discourse forced on them – was not made out of ignorance but was rather functional in ridiculing the meritocratic-orientalist trap. Ridiculing their position was in a way a way to problematise the perception that viewed underprivilegedness as a transformable character that can be changed through grades and educational achievements. The students' perception suggests that the boundaries between "good student" and "bad student" are not as fluid as some of the research suggests. Sometimes grades are not enough. In some cases, high achievements even functioned as proof of inequality because of the different/special learning process (using critical pedagogy) that the *Kedma* students went through. In these cases, the students themselves doubted their achievements and the extent to which they were "regular" and "real." In other words, the process that was seeking to unveil the role played by ethnicity and class was not enough to deconstruct social stigmatisation. While critical pedagogy assumes that academic success is a great formative force, the education process distributes various modes of identity regarding the reciprocal affinities between school and society.

The link between the school and the larger social context not only problematises the overlap between achievements and identity, between the micro level and the macro level, but also exposes the limitations of the critical process. In *Kedma*'s case, the educational achievements did contribute to the range of possibilities open to the students after graduating, both in the job market and in attaining higher education, but at the same time they exposed the students' never-ending battle regarding their self and their community's image.

7 Art education

Constrained from becoming the ideal student and at the same time driven by the critical ethics of learning, the students of *Kedma* maneuvered between hegemonic and marginalised contents offered by the school's curriculum. The Israeli schools' curriculum, in both intra- and extracurricular subject matters and activities, is governed by the national curriculum department in the Ministry of Education (*Hinuch Mamlachti*). Each subject matter has its own National Subject Superintendent (NSS) who is responsible for the production of the written materials and matriculation exams in the field and their implementation. These nationalised-institutionalised discourses and practices are embedded in various sites of learning and play an essential role in constructing the ideal subjects of the national curriculum, in light of the "image of the 'heroes' of the hegemonic Zionist narrative" (Swirski and Dagan-Buzaglo, 2011, p. 19). The teaching staff at *Kedma* attempted to combat these trends by composing a special curriculum that combined both the required national curriculum and a unique curriculum dealing with the *Mizrahi* ethnic history, culture, and social position. The students of *Kedma* were struggling with the demands of both the national curriculum and the curriculum adopted by the school. The art lessons served as a good example of these tendencies, due to the uniqueness of this subject matter, juxtaposing the Western art history canon with the national art history canon; theoretical studies and practical studies; and formal subjects and personal issues.

Art education in general, as well as in the Israeli education system, is rooted in interpretative models that have been developed in the Western thought (Bradley, 1992; Chalmers, 1999). In line with these notions, art education aims to socialise the students into consumers and producers of art in the spirit of the Western artistic canon (Bourdieu, 1984, 1993). This process is not only about teaching and learning but also about determining the students' *habitus* – the set of habits, skills, and patterns that shape and reflect a certain way of perceiving the social world and acting in the social world. In Israel, the field of art education was mainly based on the canon of Western art history, since the days of the Hebrew educational system (before '48) (Steinhardt, 2004). But despite the importance that was ascribed to Western knowledge and culture, art education remained in the margins of the national curriculum. Only during the '70s, art education underwent a process of professionalisation and even became a matriculation exam subject. Over the years, the curriculum was broadened by adding more local Israeli art works that aspired to promote the national culture and identity. The professionalisation process caused the curriculum to deflect from the national goals by putting more emphasis on cultural enrichment (Zmora Cohen, 1985), but the main goals of the program were still to acculturate students into the Western culture and the Israeli national culture. In recent years, art education in Israel has been going through numerous reforms, but despite that, the Western canon is still the most dominant characteristic of the program. It is important to note that other curriculum subjects in the field of the arts – for example: music (Cohen, 1991), theatre (Orian, 2001), and dance (Roginsky, 2009) – have been going through major multicultural changes in the last decades. The field of art is one of the only subjects that have not broadened their Eurocentric canon (Ben Zvi, 2004). Moreover, art education is almost absent from kindergartens and schools that are in low income regions (Toren, 2007). Since art education was removed from the required core curriculum in the last decade, the access of underprivileged students to art education was even reduced (Erev Rav, 2011). As the scholastic achievements of art are difficult to measure (Ronen, 1999), the subject is dismissed as not sufficiently important (Mishory, 1990); thus, art education is mainly catered to Jewish *Ashkenazi* students of privileged backgrounds.

Kedma established its art education program for students from all classes as part of the critical pedagogy adopted by the school. The art program's goals were to develop the students' awareness to their personal socio-political position and struggle, and to strengthen the ties with the culture of the local community and the *Mizrahi* culture. The school's staff members appreciated the revolutionary potential of art education; hence art education was one of the main subjects in *Kedma's* curriculum. Furthermore, since the rapid development of *Mizrachi* culture is hardly reflected in the national curriculum, incorporating *Mizrahi* art was also one of *Kedma*'s ethno-cultural goals and struggles.

The art lessons were part of the compulsory curriculum at *Kedma* from the 7th to the 12th grade. The program was divided into art history lessons and practical workshops. The art history lessons were devoted to the history and theory of art that evolved in the West and in Israel. The curriculum was designed to meet the requirements of the matriculation exams in art education. The workshops took place in a special place at the school named "the art room." The art room was a regular classroom that was converted into a studio. The actual work on the students' art was done in the art room. Thus, the students were spending a lot of time there – six-hour classes that took place every week throughout the school year. Usually the students would stay in the art room way after the official school day ended.

The art history lessons were taught by a teacher who was not part of *Kedma's* permanent teaching staff, but was invited by the school to give lectures in art history, since none of the teachers at the school were qualified to teach this subject. The workshops were conducted by Hezi, one of *Kedma's* most veteran staff member, and a much-loved teacher at the school.

Attending art education classes in *Kedma* was obligatory from 7th to 9th grade. When reaching high school (10th grade), the students could choose their major subject of learning. Specialising in art history was one of three options offered to them (the other two were theater and science). The program's requirements changed according to the level of studies. In the 12th grade the students were studying for the matriculation exams in art history. At the same time, they had to produce an artwork and a text that followed it and explained the process of production and the intentions behind it. The artwork was part of the matriculation exam. The grades on the artwork were given by an external supervisor from the department of art education. The students also curated an end-of-the-year exhibition that took place in the school's corridors and classrooms, where all the artworks would be displayed. Each year, a lot of guests visited the exhibition, among them: the students' parents and relatives, members of the community, representatives of the municipality and the department of education, and N.G.O. administrators that operated in the neighborhood. I met the students from the art lessons when they were in their 12th grade. Most of the students were Israeli-born *Mizrahi* Jews. One of the students migrated to Israel from Ethiopia and another student migrated from Georgia. All the students were living in the *Katamonin* neighborhood. Some of them suffered from economic difficulties or were under the care of welfare services. The students chose art history as their main subject. Only for a few of them art history was a default choice.

The artworks created by the students were mostly paintings (oil on canvas). Sculptures were created only by a few students using plaster casts. One student chose to create an installation made of painting, drawing, and a sculpture. Photography and video art were not offered to the students because these mediums required equipment that was too expensive for the school to handle.

In the first stages of their studies in the workshop, when I joined the class, the students were struggling with the basics of sketching and drawing on paper. In this stage the students learned how to sketch and draw and at the same time they were asked to articulate the theme of their artwork. The process of finding their own theme was not easy. The students spent weeks discussing optional subjects and contents, which were going to be part of their matriculation exam and to be exhibited in the end-of-the-year exhibition. Hezi, the art teacher, was asking the students, in the spirit of critical pedagogy, to choose a subject that would reflect personal identity/culture/social content and thus touch on the students' biographies and on the community's struggles. Contents such as this assume that articulating the personal (event, struggle, conflict, tension) is a political act, which aspires both to empower underprivileged communities and challenge the "culture of silence" that enwraps them (Freire, 1962). Aloof contents, ignoring the students' everyday life and the socio-historical conditions represent a form of further oppression (Freire and Shor, 1987). Thus, making the "subaltern speak" has become an ethical imperative in the pedagogical-political process of representation. In light of these pedagogical assumptions, Hezi was insisting that the students' personal narrative would become their main theme, and maybe even be translated in the future into social struggle (hooks, 1994). Some of the students took up the challenge and addressed topics related to their personal world: poverty, dysfunctional parents, immigration, and so on. Ami, a male student that immigrated to Israel from Georgia a few years earlier, dedicated his artwork to landscapes of the country he had left behind. Ami, lived in Georgia in a rural area. He used oil on canvas to paint the landscape, which he felt was still part of him, even though his former life was not represented in his current life. In the text accompanying his painting he wrote:

> *Missing Georgia* – I chose this title to express my homesickness for the Georgia of my childhood. My friends, relatives, the special atmosphere of the rural landscape – I've tried to convey all this forgetting the chaos we have in the neighborhood and all this violence.
>
> Markovich and Rapoport (2013b, p. 15)

Immigration was also the theme that was chosen by Elia, a male student who had immigrated to Israel from Ethiopia, together with his extended family. Elia not only gave voice to his longing for his homeland, but also criticised his immigration experience. Elia painted a large painting (oil on canvas) that addressed the negative impact the process of migration has had on the community's young generation. Elia named his painting "Childhood Landscapes." In the middle of the painting he positioned the village where he was born and raised. The text he wrote expresses the following allegations:

> In my painting I show figures from the life of the Jews in Ethiopia. I have chosen to paint a *Kes* (Jewish Ethiopian religious leader. His role was delegitimized by the Israeli rabbis) and a small boy, perhaps his son, an older man with a leather drum, and an old woman sitting at the entrance to her home. The elderly are accorded great respect in Ethiopia because they have done important things in their lives. In Israel there is less respect because Ethiopian teenagers are very influenced by Israeli society. I'd like to restore the lost honor of the elderly people of our community, and perhaps that way preserve the richness of Jewish Ethiopian tradition.
>
> Markovich and Rapoport (2013b, p. 16)

Other students also put their personal experiences, which were connected to their marginalised social position, at the center of their artwork. Nissim, a male student, was struggling between his love for soccer and becoming ultra-orthodox – a widespread phenomenon among *Mizrahim* from poor communities since *Shas* (the *Mizrahi* ultra-Orthodox party) gained a lot of influence and power. While Einat, a female student, used her painting to express her struggle with learning disabilities and her need to take a special drug to cope with her learning difficulties since early age. Einat was ascribing her hardship to her identity and culture, blaming them for her poor scholastic achievements, and at the same time being ashamed because of the help she needed. But to the teacher's surprise, not all the students were willing to cooperate with the demand to dedicate the artwork to personal-political aspects. To Hezi's surprise, a large group of students refused to ascribe their artwork to the personal-private sphere. Instead, these students preferred to emphasise universal aspects of life or general, impersonal themes. This notion should not be surprising since these themes appear frequently in modern art; therefore, the students' focus was not unusual. However, in the context of *Kedma's* critical approach, the students' rejection was exceptional. The students explained their preference by using terms that indicated that they were more drawn to internal expressions. Tammy, a female student, said: "Painting is about my intimate feeling," and Ossi, a female student, said: "Art is something from the inside." This notion emphasises individualism rather than the individual as a political phenomenon. Even though expressing the inner parts of the self by using art's tool box is widespread among artists (Ofrat, 1987), the students' choice to address these topics was given a different meaning. Efrat, a female student, said:

> I don't want to always deal with the [...] I mean... students from good schools [privileged students] don't talk about their life and ethnicity and... they choose to make art about whatever they want to.

Efrat was framing the personal-political aspects as a content and practice that were designed mainly for underprivileged students. In her view, dealing with the ethnic background drew a clear boundary between students from different social and economic strata. Yossi, a male student, also claimed that the content/practice offered to the students during their art studies was labeling them as students in need:

> All the time this is the thing that they (the school) talk about. Our identity and the community and the, the way we are in the margins. It is only, this stuff is only for us. It's like a symbol of us.

By understanding ethnicity and class, and the critical pedagogy of narrating them, as a content-praxis that is directed only toward underprivileged students, the students of *Kedma* understood this content-praxis as a tool that exposed their underprivilegedness, rather than as a tool that empowered them. In other words, the critical pedagogy's praxis was perceived as a labeling mechanism. The students' resistance to personal narration was further explained by Rami, a male student:

> I'm not into it. I prefer to dedicate my [art]work to different issues. I want to paint the sea. I love the ocean... I love the sound of the sea and... and my experience in the sea. Why is it always that we [the people living in poor neighborhoods] are attached only to our homes (place of living)?

For Rami, choosing personal content that is embedded in the community means anchoring himself only to one meaning. This meaning is perceived as reductive and even as reproducing reductiveness. Ossi, a female student, was also de-naturalising the common beliefs ascribed to critical pedagogy, claiming that identifying with critical pedagogy highlighted her inferiority:

> It is not natural to do something (artwork) on my problems. You don't go and talk about your problem, you know, about things that don't put you and your community in a good light. I want to do what other students do in their art classes.

For Ossi, the national curriculum plays a normalising role. Not adjusting to the regular contents and practices was perceived by her as a second marginalisation. A marginalisation that was performed with the approval of the critical content.

Defining both narratives – the national and that of the school – as routes for marginalisation exposed the gap between the students' ethnic-class position and the formal national rhetoric. For the majority of students, the interplay between their ethnic-class narrative and the Western oriented and national narrative was further reinforcing their marginalised social position. Thus, in the students' views, both curricular routes reflected the division between them and the privileged students. Even though the high school's art curriculum suggests a process of knowledge production that combines the dominant Western knowledge together with intrinsic personal knowledge, underprivileged ethnic-class narratives were not considered as a legitimate knowledge in most of the students' views. Revealing the juxtaposition between the national and the personal curriculum as a slippery slope position did not leave the students a path to detach their identity from undermining labels. Being unable to fully identify with the national curriculum but refusing to apply an ethnic language that would emphasise their particularity, the students kept navigating between the available compartmentalisations – "insider"/"outsider."

8 The annual school trip

Relying on the assumption that the classroom comprises only one site of learning and that ethnicity and nationality can be traced more easily in locations that are characterised by myths and rituals, I decided to join the obligatory annual school trip. The Israeli school trip has unique history and characteristics. The chronology of the local national hiking tradition dates back to the beginning of the Zionist movement's activities in *Eretz Israel*. The first organised field trips started as early as 1903 in order to facilitate national meanings through the physical engagement with the land, a phenomenon known as "conquering the land through the feet" [in Hebrew: "להכיר את הארץ ברגליים"] (Schama, 1995). The field trips were founded by a few teachers that belonged to the European Zionist pioneers (Margolin, 1947; Haramati, 2000) that laid the foundations for the dominant *Ashkenazi* national culture. Blending together socialism, nationalism, and pantheism – ideas that were widespread in the national youth movements in Europe (Fisher, 1959; Springhall, 1977) – the field trips aimed to connect the hikers to the land (Almog, 2000). To develop a feeling of belonging, the students had to overcome difficult, and sometimes dangerous, excursions that were supposed to strengthen their body and their patriotic feelings. By doing that, the field trip wished to destroy the image of the diasporic Jew, who was portrayed as a helpless, humiliated, and defeated human being (Shapira, 1997), and reconstruct the ideal "New Jew." But the hiking students not only had to incorporate the national ideas, the national ideas were also incorporated into the land, turning the field trip into a mechanism of "territorial fetishism" (Mitchell, 1994). The flora and fauna (Zerubavel, 1995), topography (Bar-Gal, 1993), archaeology (Feige and Shiloni, 2008), and Bible studies (Shapira, 2005) were all recruited in order to attach national significance to *Eretz Israel* in line with the *Ashkenazi* pioneers' culture. In other words, the national ideology was carved in the mountains and wadis that constituted the trip's path. In Lefebvre's (1991) terms, geography was marked by ideology. During this process, some parts of the land are constructed as "absolute spaces," that represent the unifying symbolic nature of the nation. This process, that may be considered as "geographical violence," is produces by the hegemonic national group through various cultural methods that have been invented in order to conceptualise the national ideology and mediate it to the students through the land. Among them are guided landscape observation, game-like activities, and even navigation. Hence, the annual school trip has become an integral part of the Israeli education system and a compulsory activity for all grades from kindergarten through the end of high school (Director General's Communiqué, 2005). Even though in the last decade the annual school trip has suffered from too many attractions (State Comptroller, 1996), violence, and inadequate behavior (Poltin, 2009), the ideological aims of the school trip have remained relatively the same (Gertel, 2002).

I joined the annual school trip of 12th-grade students as one of the travelers. The trip lasted three full days. We met at the school early in the morning, waiting for the bus and the tour guide, that were hired by the school, to arrive. We only left the school hours later because some of the students were extremely late. Even though we were behind schedule, the tour guide decided to stick to the plan, and so we were heading from Jerusalem to the northern parts of Israel. Late at noon we started hiking along a stream located in a steep wadi in the Golan Heights. We spent the night in a guest house in a Kibbutz in the area. On the second day we hiked in a nature reserve that has a natural grove and a waterfall. In the evening we had a cruise and a party on one of the little boats that hosts tourists in the Sea of Galilee. We spent the third day in a water park near the Jordan Valley. This day was dedicated to fun and relaxation. In the afternoon we started the long bus journey back home to Jerusalem. The staff members that joined the trip included five homeroom teachers, three subject teachers, a medic, a qualified tour guide, and the bus driver. All the staff members were Jews except for the bus driver – a Palestinian living in east Jerusalem. All the participants were *Mizrahin*, except for the tour guide and me – the only *Ashkenazim* on board. Despite the difficulties we faced before we actually hit the road, all the staff members were enthusiastic. The school trip was the students' last trip, hence symbolising not just the end-of-the-year celebrations but also the students' last year in the education system, and their last year in what they called "home" – the *Kedma* school.

The staff was in high spirits, but the students did not stop complaining from day one. They were angry about the long hike, about the warm weather, about the mosquitos, and about the tour guide's demands. Complaining, breaking the school rules, and challenging the hierarchy between students and teachers during school trips are considered the norm by a lot of high school students. Being a kind of a liminal space, the annual school trip even serves as a platform that allows to experience trial and error and to resist the formal system (Kahane, 2007). Despite these notions, I would suggest that the students in *Kedma* systematically challenged the trip's features and cultural characters, not as part of the naughtiness and pranks ascribed to teenagers. In many instances, the students' behavior was a kind of resistance to the cultural narratives and praxis that the annual school trip imposed. The students challenged the annual school trip's customs by using their ethnic-class identity and culture. By doing that, they addressed the cultural mode of the trip that they identified and labeled as *Ashkenazi*, meaning as totally different from their own culture.

The first clash between the students and the school trip's patterns occurred when the students were asked by the tour guide on the first day of the trip to start hiking the long trail down the wadi. The students refused to get off the bus. Only after an intense argument with the teachers, and after the teachers forbade them to stay on the bus, did the students unwillingly begin the trek. Soon after the students started hiking, they also began to challenge the pattern of hiking in various ways:

SHLOMI (MALE STUDENT): Are there snakes here?

AVI (MALE STUDENT): Are you mad? I'm not going to get down that wadi.

GUIDE: But it is not so difficult, watch me.

EFI (MALE STUDENT): Cut it out. We're not Ashkenazi pioneers. You know, times have changed. Maybe you haven't noticed but we do not live in the '30s (of the twentieth century) anymore... Maybe he will also ask us to build a Kibbutz or dry a swamp [the students are laughing].

GUIDE: Come on, get serious, we must continue walking. It's a trip, and during trips one should walk.

SARAH (FEMALE STUDENT): No, we shouldn't. Why did you bring us here? We could have done something [another route] which is much nicer and easier. Now how do I get across? Is there a shortcut?

Markovich (2016, p. 244–245)

The students kept comparing their performance to that of the imagined pioneers. Even though the pioneer period has long gone, the pioneers served as the students' main reference point. The students were not just referring to the pioneers' image but also to the role ascribed to them in the *Ashkenazi* Zionist history. The pioneers' main roles were to conquer the land both by building new settlements and by drying the swamps that spread mainly in the northern parts of *Palestine/Eretz Israel*. These were some of the most important, and sometimes dangerous, activities that became a myth in the Israeli national culture. In other words, the students re-contextualised the annual school trip by using ethnic signifiers. These signifiers served to stress the ideological aspects and history of the annual school trip, as well as the ways the students divested from this history. The students' laughter after comparing themselves to the pioneers manifested not only the difference between these two ethnic groups/cultures, but also the students' relatively inferior social position. Furthermore, by assuming that they do not fit in this cultural (as well as actual) route, the students affirmed that their main cultural resources were not part of the national culture and identity. On another occasion, the students challenged the *Ashkenazi* concept of travelling by mocking the tour guide's instructions, which were as follows:

> Everybody, are you ready to go? Let's start walking. We must keep on walking at a good speed. We have to be able to continue [...] We cannot stop every few minutes. You must follow me and listen. Look at the nature around you, look how lovely everything is. Does it even interest you? It's also your country.

The tour guide repeated the "right" ways of travelling. These patterns included the "right" pace, the "right" determination, and the "right" interest in the land. But the students refused to cooperate with the annual school trip's mode of hiking, as it was reflected in the guide's rhetorical question ("does it even interest you?"). The guide's rhetorical question also reflected an implied accusation regarding the students' attitude toward the landscape, and thus toward the land. This hint became evident later, when the students reached the bottom of the wadi:

RINA (FEMALE STUDENT): I will never be able to climb up this thing. I swear to god that I will never ever, ever, go to this kind of trip again.

BELLA (FEMALE STUDENT): It's a nightmare. A nightmare!

GUIDE: It is your country, your land, your views. Don't you admire it? Don't you appreciate walking here and absorbing all this beauty? You know how hard we fought to be able to hike here?

The guide was struck by the students' responses to the concept of the trip. For him, as a professional representative of the annual school trip, to travel the land means to love the land. This equation constructed a one-to-one connection between the physical and the emotional dimensions of the trip, between the corporeal and ideological. Moreover, the guide also suggested that by rejecting this equation, the students rejected any national sentiment. For him, constructing national feelings toward the land was a process that was mediated through the trip. Negating the trip could have only one meaning – negating the national identity. The national narrative, and especially the national culture, was perceived by the tour guide as a general and only narrative/culture, rather than a narrative/culture that represents a specific Jewish ethnic group – that of the *Ashkenazim*. But in the students' view, if the word nationalism meant anything, it implied the dominant *Ashkenazi* ways of loving the land. Thus, the students' different behavior and attitudes were portrayed against this unmarked *Ashkenazi* national culture.

The students' ethnic resistance was visible also in relation to the trip's historical narrative. The history of the places that the students visited was presented by the tour guide and the teachers during the hikes and during the long bus rides. The narratives were centered on two points in the history of the land: the biblical period – this part of the ideological sites of the national socialisation was underpinning the walking trail, and the Zionist period. The biblical period emphasised the main events that happened to the *People of Israel*, while the Zionist period emphasised the main events that happened to the Jewish people. Maneuvering between these two eras enabled to illustrate the continuity of the Israelites in the Promised Land for over 2000 years. But this narrative did not impress the students. The tour guide's efforts to persuade the students to adopt this narrative, and to identify themselves through this narrative, were unsuccessful:

GUIDE: Listen guys, listen, be quiet [...] I want to tell you the history of this place since Abraham was here... Guys, can you please shut up? Hey guys, I'm talking to you. Try to imagine yourselves here in the last century... trying to combat all the enemies that threatened Israel... try to put yourselves in their position. How we, the Israelis, acted in those days. How we as Israelis stood together and didn't surrender.

MEIR (MALE STUDENT): But we are not fighters, we are the cooks [the students burst with a huge laughter]

The guide was trying to embrace all the students under one unifying national story by referring to them as Israelis ("we the Israelis"). The collective term – Israelis – implied that there is only one kind of Israeli, rather than several versions of Israelis. This kind of Israeli was described through a narrative that highlighted his/her patriotic devotion on the battlefield. But the students could not relate to this example, and thus did not pay respect to this narrative. Instead, they kept talking together with the tour guide, disrupting his efforts to get their attention. In the end, Meir's remark blew up the guide's patriotic narrative. Not only did the students not personalise the national narrative and make it their own, they also reframed the national narrative within their different ethic-class position. We are not the kind of soldiers that fight on the battlefield, they said. We are the cooks – those soldiers that give services, and thus are positioned in the lowest strata of the military's division of labor. This ethnic-class contextualisation marked the students as the outsiders of the much-praised Israeli soldier, even though the students are Jews, Zionist, and take part in military service. Being the "Others from within" (Alcalay, 1987), as opposed, for example, to the status of the Palestinians living in Israel, who are considered as "outsiders," the students felt that they could not connect to this national narrative and to the national culture of traveling in this narrative's footsteps. The incongruity between the structural and ideological determinants of the annual school trip and the students' social-class position aroused not just conflicting discourses, but also responses that generated new types of knowledge. This knowledge strived to "ethnicise" the trip's modes and patterns in various ways, thus widening the national cultural repertoires that the annual school trip suggested. These attempts were evident in a few cases when the students tried to cross the national culture's symbolic boundaries and reshape them. On the third day of the trip, during lunch break, the students started to transform the trip into their way of spending time in nature:

ELI (MALE STUDENT): Yalla (a word in Arabic that is used for goading) let's eat, I'm starving.
AVI (MALE STUDENT): Put here all the stuff we bought: the pita bread, the salads, the humus [...] we'll open everything so everyone will have access to the food like we do when we have a barbecue on Independence Day
LEVI (MALE STUDENT): Yeah... Let's imagine that we are in the park celebrating with the family and the guys from the neighborhood, like we, Kurdish people, do.

BENNY (MALE STUDENT): Yalla, yalla, turn up the *Mizrachi* music [one of the students is using his hands to imitate a big amplifier which has supposedly been turned on]

YAKI (MALE STUDENT) starts singing a famous Mizrahi song. The students join him loudly

ELI (MALE STUDENT): Come on bring the nargila (Arabic water pipe), bring it closer to us [some students carry an imagined nargila and "smoke" it, moving it from one to the other]. I swear, it's like being in a khafla (Arabic word for an event that includes eating and singing. In Hebrew khafla is attributed to the *Mizrahi* culture and thus perceived as characterizing simplicity and even vulgarity)

AVI (MALE STUDENT): You know what, now that really feels like celebrating Independence Day, you were right [...] you just sit like that in the park, eating, laughing, having fun [...]

LEVI (MALE STUDENT): You don't have to climb any mountains ha [laughing]. You can love your country from the park, didn't have to do it from a cliff [they are all laughing]

Markovich (2016, p. 248)

The students were turning the annual school trip into a kind of outdoor activity that was more familiar to them. This imagined activity created a different mode of "traveling," by using language and practices that the students ascribed to their community (see also Barur Ben-David, 1998). There are several traditional *Mizrahi* holidays that are celebrated in parks. Among them: the *Mimouna* – brought by Jewish immigrants from North African, the *Seharane* – brought by Jewish immigrants from Kurdistan (see: Sharaby, 2011; Sabar, 1989), and Independence Day. While the *Mimouna* and the *Seharane* migrated to Israel during the 1950s, having a *khafla* and barbequing meat in national parks during Independence Day is a local invented tradition ascribed mostly to *Mizrahim*. This ritual that combines ethnicity, masculinity, and patriotism was even named as "grilled nationalism" (Avieli, 2013). The students applied these labeled cultural features and characteristics to the annual school trip. By doing that the students were not only referring to familiar traditions, but also mocked the trip's structure and goals. Thus, the students mocking did not express negative emotions toward the national goals of the trip, and especially the trip's patriotic discourse. On the contrary, the students emphasised their positive feelings and emotions toward the national identity by pointing out Independence Day as a day of celebration. But despite their connection to the national discourse/identity, the students transformed the national culture expressed by the annual school trip into a parody. This specific kind of parody juxtaposed Arabic slang, traditions, and habits with the Zionist field trip, creating a hybrid event that defamiliarised the need to climb a mountain in order to become part of the national collective. The sense of national belonging, the students insisted, can be gained through different cultural routes than that of the *Ashkenazi* national culture.

In different event that occurred during the last day of the school trip, the students further expressed their different ethnic-class position by using a lexicon that expressed quite a different outdoor experience:

[Excerpt from the field notes] We are heading to our last destination on this trip – The water-park. The students have been waiting for this part impatiently. They kept asking the teachers to cancel the other parts of the trip and dedicate the rest of the trip's time to having 'fun'. Now, the bus is full of laughter and joy. The students are singing aloud a well-known song that was performed by a legendary *Mizrahi* singer from Yemenite origin. The singer was a heroin addict for years. He died tragically after committing suicide while staying in a detention cell after being arrested for possessing drugs. The students invented new words for the song. One of them accompanies the singing by playing a darbuka, an Arabic drum, another is leading the singing, and the others are repeating the tune.

LEAD SINGER (MALE STUDENT): What are we doing here?
CHOIR: What are we doing here?
LEAD SINGER: We are stuck on the school's trip
CHOIR: We are stuck on the school's trip
LEAD SINGER: Who can save us from the school's trip?
CHOIR: Who can save us from the school's trip?
LEAD SINGER: We are the Arabs of this trip
CHOIR: We are the Arabs of this trip
LEAD SINGER: At the end of the ladder
CHOIR: At the end of the ladder.

Ascribing the term "Arabs" to Jews represents the ultimate rejection of the Zionist identity created by the *Ashkenazi* hegemony. The de-Arabisation project, conducted by the European-oriented Zionist model/image, is not tolerant of mixtures like this. As local residents, the students were aware of the Arabs' position in the Israeli society, as it was reflected in the resemblance they drew between their marginality on the trip and that of the Arabs ("at the end of the ladder"). Thus, the comparison made in the lyrics invented by the students was neither a slip of the tongue nor a discursive provocation. The students not only compared their status in the national culture (the annual school trip) to that of the Arabs, but also identified themselves as Arabs ("we are the Arabs of this trip"). By doing that, they opposed the Zionist homogenisation project in various ways. First, this opposition was shedding light on locations in the Zionist project that marginalised Jews in the same way they marginalised non-Jews. Second, by declaring: "We are the Arabs of this trip," the students said loudly that they do not have a place in these traditions and cannot have a place in these traditions. Even though the students are included in the Zionist identity/group, at the same time they felt that they are excluded by the cultural mechanisms of this identity/group. This inclusion-exclusion praxis (Forum, 2002) is a simultaneous process that strives both to construct a united national collective, and to label those who do not fit in. Being parts of a group that do not and cannot fit, the students wished to transform the trip's modes into something that they could relate to. The water park – a location that presents a global mode of leisure – was thus the preferred way for spending time together, even though, and maybe because, it was detached from any national meaning.

The events that singled out aspects of ethnicity during the annual school trip were contesting, and in some cases reshaping, the national culture. The interface between nationality and ethnicity thus did not illustrate possible bridges between the two, but rather the strategies the students used in order to cope with this rift. The dominance of the ethnic factor points to the dominance of ethnicity in the students' self and collective perception, due to their marginalised and labeled position. This position was generating a sense of unsuitableness and thus of resistance. The students' discomfort within the dominant national culture infused the trip with different modes of behavior and attitude, even when those were made of symbolic and imagined gestures. However, these acts were not about formulating radical alternatives to the national identity, or to nationality as a whole. The students did not wish to change their national affiliation or to relinquish it. Hence, the boundary crossings made by the students were not about negating the Zionist idea. The students' transgression can be understood as a way of normalisation, i.e., as a different way to belong. Suggesting that there are different ways one can demonstrate his national belonging is suggesting that the *Ashkenazi* national culture is just an option. This suggestion de-legitimised not just the dominance of the *Ashkenazi* option, but also, in a way, the East/West dichotomy it imposes. Furthermore, the very existence of the Zionist categorisation assumes that there are various other options of nationalism that need to be overcome. The students' reactions gave these different ethnic-class

approaches to the national culture visibility, opening a path of participation that did not position the students apart from the "Israeliness."
Evolving in the cracks between the national feelings and the way they
were culturally preformed, they challenged the dominant terms of belonging and processes of hegemonisation while trying to widen the
boundaries of acceptance into the national narrative/identity. Dyeing
the national culture with a unique ethnic shade was also manifested
during the boundary work done by the students and staff in the organisation of the Day of Remembrance for the Fallen Soldiers.

9 The national Memorial Day for the fallen soldiers

The *Kedma* school's memorial service for the fallen soldiers was part of Israel's national Memorial Day. The national Memorial Day for the Fallen Soldiers (*Yom HaZikaron* in Hebrew) represents a special, and even sacred, civil religion event in the Jewish-Israeli national culture. Remembrance Day is held a day before Independence Day. A two-minute siren, sounded throughout Israel, and flags that are lowered to half-mast, symbolise the official start of the ceremonies. When the sirens are wailing, a synchronic commemoration takes place in many parts of Israel. For 24 hours, all places of public entertainment are closed in order to express their sadness and grief, while radio and television stations broadcast only programs dedicated to the fallen soldiers.

Remembrance Day commemorates the fallen Israel Defense Forces (IDF) soldiers that were killed in action, as well as soldiers that died of various reasons while serving in the army. In recent years, the definition of the victims to be commemorated has been widened to include also civilians that were killed in acts of hostility. However, the Memorial Day ceremonies avoid hierarchies as well as differences between wars, battles, and events. All those who lost their lives are commemorated in the same way, despite the differences in ranks, roles, and circumstances of death. This concept of unity and equality was forced on the ceremonies in order to blur discords regarding war, and to blur the socio-political tensions in the Israeli society, and thus to sustain collective boundaries (Weiss, 1997). The fact that Israel is still embedded in an on-going conflict, and the harsh debate that accompanies this fact and, sometimes, reflects the differences in the Israeli society (right/left, *Mizrahim/Ashkenazim*, Jews/Palestinians living in Israel), contributed to the desire to leave differences outside of the ceremony's gates. Since one of the main roles ascribed to the ceremony is to articulate past and present, in order to construct a powerful national identity and ensure the future of the nation, the rituals present a narrative that can be recognised by everyone. But, despite this mix of memory and forgetfulness, and despite the claims for unity, the traditional ceremony conducted in Israel reflects the *Ashkenazi* pioneers' Zionist culture (Renan, [1882] 1990). From a historical point of view, the commemorative work and ceremonies can be traced back to the *Yishuv* period, when the *Ashkenazi* pioneers set the cultural tone. Hence, the events still emphasise the image of the farmer and the soldier and their "*Sabra*" offspring, and the crucial contribution they made to the national rebirth. Ideologically, these ceremonies echo the pioneers' views, leaning mostly on narratives that highlight their obligation to the Zionist collective (Ben-Amos and Bet-El, 1999). It is important to note that the Memorial Day is accompanied by other strategies that strive to embed the memory in the everyday, "natural," un-questioned banal nationalism life settings (Billig, 1995). These strategies include utilisation of street names for commemoration (Azaryahu, 1996a); Monuments that express the geography of the public memory materially (Ben-Amos, 2003); Heritage sites that activate national memory by adding political iconography to the local topography (Katriel, 1994); Cemeteries that become state shrines (Azaryahu, 1996b); and architectural objects that narrate the national memory through their structural text (Yacobi, 2008). As mentioned above, this spatial symbolic fabric that dot the landscape, consolidates into one specific memorial time-space during the annual ceremony.

The schools' Remembrance Day ceremony is a ritual constructed by the Ministry of Education in order to preserve and bequeath the national ethos and collective memory. Beside the annual ceremony, most high schools have a "memorial corner" exhibiting the names and photos of fallen graduates. The canon of the ceremony, as it was constructed by the Ministry of Education, takes place outdoors in front of an audience that includes the school's staff, students, and guests. The ceremony is conducted by the students, who usually wear white shirts with a sticker of a poppy seed. The ceremony includes a mixture of national and religious gestures, including: lowering the national flag, reading the *Yizkor* prayer, lighting memorial candles, and singing the national anthem. The other parts of the ceremony are staged by the school authorities. The school authorities have the freedom to decide the repertoire of speeches, readings, and songs that will be part of the school's ceremony. Even though choosing the repertoire is each school's decision, the Ministry of Education and other organisations publish booklets that limit the memorial repertoire selection by presenting the canonical national narrative. Most of the materials included in the repertoire echo the *Ashkenazi* culture, which is much praised and is even

known as representing the "beautiful *Eretz Israel*" ("ארץ ישראל היפה").
This repertoire consists mainly of essays, songs, and poetry emphasising the contribution of the fallen soldiers to the state of Israel, and
the big debt we, the living, owe them ("the dead have bequeathed us
life"). Even though in the last decade the national bereavement culture
and ceremonies have faced private, unauthorised, and spontaneous
attempts of mourning (Bilu and Witztum, 2000) as well as elements
of innovation (Lomsky-Feder, 2004), these changes mostly reflect the
Ashkenazi middle class. Thus, these new communities of memory do
not deflect from the mode and structure of mourning conducted by the
Ashkenazi national culture. More than these changes criticise the national culture or give voice to alternative multi-vocal narratives, they
are driven by, and reproduce, both the privileged position of the dominant groups and the hegemonic national culture.

As one of the important components that shape the national identity,
the rituals were conducted in *Kedma* each year with a group of selected
students. The ceremony started at 11:00 AM in the school yard. In the
minutes before the siren started wailing one could feel the bustle in
the air. Last arrangements took place on the improvised stage while
the audience, composed of students and teachers, started gathering
and taking their places. The last beeping sounds from the microphones
were still cutting through the air when the powerful siren got everyone
to their position on stage. The siren lasted for two minutes. The crowd
stood in *heavy silence*, gazing at the gap between their feet. Nobody
dared to interrupt this powerful moment, when students and teachers,
teenagers and adults, become one. Only when the siren started to fade
did rustlings invade the silence. But these seconds of liminality soon
cleared when one of the students lit up the torch and another student
started to declaim the *Yizkor* prayer. After the prayer ended and the
crowd said "Amen," the school's part of the ceremony began. This part
was composed of an eclectic collection of speeches, chorus, reading
passages, and an abstract dance. All the readings and singings echoed
the hegemonic *Ashkenazi* bereavement culture. Only when this part
ended, the students started to sing medleys of famous *Mizrahi* songs.

Kedma's ceremony stood out from the traditional ceremony by re-
interpreting the dimensions of time and space that characterise the national commemorative culture. The ceremonial time is a multifaceted
dimension, since time is being represented by both linear and circular
tracks. While the linear track follows the historical chronology of the
national wars, the circular track loads the ceremony and the nation with
a sacred-mythical dimension that is not affected by the passage of time
(Eliade, 1963). The manifestation of present and eternity as a neutral

flow is gained through this jamming, which mixes together battles and wars, eras and periods, blood and blood. This manipulation creates a timeless "time zone" that emphasises the war as an ongoing and necessary motif in the Israeli existence and thus turns the ceremony into a national martyrology (Zerubavel, 1995). The circular manipulation of past and present is also a common feature in the traditional school ceremony. Like the formal national ceremonies, the school ceremonies transform various events that ended in death into a coherent collective memory. This collective memory strives to strengthen the moral claims over the land, while turning the land into a sacred place due to the soldiers that were buried in it. The ceremony conducted by *Kedma* deviated from this mode. Even though the school's ceremony seemed to highlight various military events and merge them into one stapled symbolic event, the composition of the events combined together was different, including: The *First Lebanon war*, the *Second Intifada (Al-Aqsa)*, Ron Arad's captivity, the IDF soldiers lynched in Ramallah, and the suicide attack on bus number 32A in Jerusalem. At first glance, it looks like *Kedma's* ceremony plays into the hands of the traditional ceremony by constructing a continuous line of military activities that stretches from '48 to the present day. As in the traditional national ceremony, the event has featured burning tanks, fighters that crossed the enemy lines, and pilots in dangerous missions. But a careful look will reveal that this compressed heroic time splits into lanes of memory that are usually silenced in the formal ceremonies. Beside the mythological events mentioned, the students were also mentioning civilian events, failed missions, controversial military events, and non-heroic events. This was the case of the *Second Intifada* – a war that took place on the civilian home front and confronted Palestinian civilians with Israeli civilians. The case of the *First Lebanon war*, which caused one of the biggest public debates and controversies in ways that had not been spoken out loud in Israel until then; the case of Ron Arad – an Israeli Air Force weapon system officer (WSO) who was lost in a mission over Lebanon on 16 October 1986, captured by the *Amal* group, tortured, and is still classified as missing in action. And the case of the violent incident that took place on 12 October 2000 at the *el-Bireh* police station, where a Palestinian crowd killed and mutilated the bodies of two Israel Defense Forces immigrant reservist soldiers who had accidently entered the Palestinian Authority-controlled era. The picture of Aziz Salha, one of the lynchers, waving his hands, covered with the soldiers' blood, at the crowds that gathered in front of the station, became one of the most traumatic images in Israel. The last event that was mentioned in *Kedma's* ceremony was the number

32A bus bombing. The bus blew-up in *Pat* junction (a few meters from the *Kedma* school), due to a suicide attack carried out by the Palestinian Islamic group *Hamas* on 18 June 2002. The bomber blew himself up in the bus by activating an explosive belt that included metal balls in order to maximise casualties. Nineteen people were killed and 74 were wounded, some of them severely. The casualties of most of these events – the *Second Intifada*, the lynching, and the bus bombing – were soldiers and civilians from the periphery of Israel.

How were meanings read into these events that represent non-heroic time-zones? "Let's be honest," said Oren, one of the teachers that organised the ceremony, "People from the neighborhood don't participate in combat military service. We don't have any battle heritage here, and this is why the kids [the students] are not connected to these stories." Oren claimed that most of *Kedma's* students, like other youths in the neighborhood, do not serve in elite units in the IDF. From this fact he concludes that their national sentiment is mainly attached to local events rather than heroic national events. "Most of the people that were injured here [in the neighborhood] were injured during suicide bombings and not in the battlefield. This is what occupies peoples' minds here." Oren is hinting in his words at the division of labor in the IDF, and thus the division of commemoration in the national Israeli culture. *Mizrahim* from lower classes usually serve in service-oriented units – transport, munition, and feeding. These units are perceived in the Israeli society as "blue collar" jobs, hence they are much less prestigious than those of the fighters from the combat units. In contrast, middle class *Ashkenazim* constitute the largest part of the fighters of the combat units, and thus portray the hegemonic soldier prototype (Lomsky-Feder and Ben Ari, 1999). This social order/mechanism does not just affect the army, but reflects and reproduces a stratified mode of belonging to the Israeli state, since being a combat soldier also represents "good citizenship" according to the republican conception (Sasson-Levy, 2002). The *Kedma* students and graduates deviated from the *Ashkenazi* masculine order/model; hence their ability to exchange the military service for better social positioning was limited. Thus, being a victim, for example, of a suicide bomb attack that struck the lower classes that use public transportation, is one of the only resources available to them (on the changes in the social composition of casualties see: Levy, 2006). Oren proceeded to claim: "We don't have witnesses from the battlefield. We cannot share here first-hand experiences of the heroic type." From Oren's point of view, the peripheralisation of the composition of casualties – who in Enloe's words (1980) were sacrificed – is reshaping the bereavement culture as well as the ways it is articulated in the ceremonies. Oren insists that without the symbolic capital of an authentic-personal report from the battlefield, the *Kedma* ceremony must rely on non-heroic times of war, where the main heroes are women, children, and elderly people that got on a bus, or fallen immigrants that served as reservist soldiers, or those who participated in de-legitimised wars. Avi, another teacher who helped organise the ceremony, explained: "We operate in different times [...] Those of the community's biography." The wars of the social peripheries, said Avi, happened in a different time-zone, that of the local-patriots from the neighborhood. But, despite their different positioning, the people from the neighborhood also wished to be considered as being recruited, dispatched, and buried in the name of the nation. This phenomenon – the "militarisation" of the civilian deaths – thus both serves the national discourse, and doubts the canonic cultural discourse by placing the "Other" battlefields at the center of the national event. These "Other" battlefields, which were positioned on the bus, in the Israeli peripheral roads, and in the Palestinian streets, can be described as "in between" battlefield – in between "nationality" and "ethnicity."

A different way of belonging was also manifested through the *Kedma* ceremony's soundtrack. Music plays a pivotal role in the process of nation building (Anderson, 2006). The symbolic power of music is perceived as both establishing the cultural boundaries of the nation and safeguarding them, in a non-salient manner. This component of nationality has a significant contribution in times of crisis. Thus, music plays a major part in ceremonies in general and in school ceremonies in particular. The music that is played in Israeli memorial ceremonies, and hence the cultural code that defines and re-affirms the local collective sound-trek, has been mostly composed and performed in accordance with the *Ashkenazi* pioneers' Eastern-European-oriented culture (Kaplan, 2009). By using these hegemonic national songs and musical performances, the ceremony is recreating a kind of "national *communitas*," as Liron, one of the teachers, explained: "This music [*Ashkenazi* music] [...] we were socialized on these sounds. Whenever I hear this music, they are [the *Ashkenazi* songs] our inalienable assets." In Liron's words, the music that encompasses meanings of nationhood and togetherness in the Zionist context is of a specific kind. This kind of music activates her emotions and makes her feel that she is part of a collective. By contrast, *Mizrahi* music occupies the opposite pole of the Israeli culture. *Mizrahi* music (*Musika Mizrahit* in Hebrew), also called "Mediterranean music," is a genre that combines Arab elements from both Asian and North African origins and is performed by *Mizrahi* artists (usually in Hebrew). *Mizrahi* music was rejected for years by the Eurocentric Israeli music industry and *Ashkenazi* audience, due to its Arabic sound and style (Horowitz, 1999). Being very popular among *Mizrahim*, and being partly accepted in the Israeli culture, after an ongoing struggle, this genre started to reset the boundaries of the national culture (Regev, 2000). But despite these changes, and to this day, the *Mizrahi* music that commingles with Arab sounds and lyrics is incorporated in the Israeli culture only as a means of reinforcing Zionism (Saada-Ophir, 2006). In light of this, the hegemony of the *Ashkenazi* music that is usually played in the ceremonies gained different meanings for some of the teachers. Sagi, a staff member who participated in the meeting that preceded the ceremony, said in response: "It [the music played in the ceremonies] tells sad stories. But I wouldn't listen to this music if it wasn't for the ceremony." Sagi's response points to the difference between the content of the musical pieces played in the ceremonies and his personal musical practice. The ceremony in *Kedma* tried to bridge this gap between ceremonial events and everyday life, between East and West, by merging into a different narrative after repeating the traditional canonised part. The ceremony started with a series of *Ashkenazi* hegemonic melodies and songs: *"We're from the same village"* ("אנחנו מאותו הכפר"), which was written by one of the Israeli national song writers – Naomi Shemer (1966). The song tells the story of two soldiers from the same village that had similar characters and were good friends, until one of them found his death in the war; "All we pray for" ("לו יהי") was also written by Naomi Shemer (1973). The song was dedicated to the *Yom Kippur* fallen soldiers and became an Israeli anthem striving for peace and quiet in the land; "The middle of Tammuz" (the tenth month in the Hebrew calendar)" ("אמצע התמוז") was also written by Naomi Shemer (1979). The song portrays the heavy clouds of deep grief and sorrow caused by the waste of life; "Each of us has a name" ("לכל איש שם") was written by the poet Zelda (Zelda Schneersohn Mishkovsky) (1974). The song deals with remembrance and the ways we, as a collective, should remember all those who left, never to return, victims of the gas chambers and the war. Only after these mournful songs, which were sung by two solo student-singers, the ceremony proceeded to a series of *Mizrahi* songs. The *Mizrahi* medley included the songs: "The fruits from your garden" ("פרי גנך") written by Yoni Roeh (1989). The song tells the story of a mother that waits for her dead son to return home from the army service. A wish that will never be fulfilled. The song was written after Roeh met the mother of one of his classmates that was killed in an operational accident while serving in the army; "When the heart cries" ("כשהלב בוכה"), written by Yossi Gispan (2009). The song is dedicated to the soldiers that found their cruel death in the lynch in Ramallah; and "Mama's soldier" ("חייל של אימא"), written by Lior Narkis (2011), which tells the story of a son that doesn't return home from his base to his worried, expecting mom.

These songs, chosen for the *Kedma* ceremony, transformed the event into a field of negotiation that maneuvered between two poles: that of the traditional bereavement culture and that of the *Mizrahi* culture. This musical repertoire echoes the social and political transformation that has taken place in Israel, while each pole calibrates to a different period. The *Ashkenazi* songs refer to the heroic wars that raged until the '80s (*"48 War," "Six Days War," "Yom Kippur War"*). These wars were perceived by the Israeli society as horrible events that were forced on it by the Arab world in order to demolish the Israeli state. Despite the heavy losses they caused, these wars were perceived as "non-choice" wars, and thus gained the public's legitimation. During this period, and until 1977, Israel was ruled by the *Labor party* – the only hegemony at that time – which was composed mostly of the *Ashkenazi* group (Kimmerling, 2001; Almog, 2004). As opposed to this period, the *Mizrahi* songs refer to the wars that took place since the '80s (the first and second *Intifada*, and the era of the suicide bombings). These wars were perceived by parts of the Israeli society as wars that were a result of political interests, and thus could be avoided or resolved by using diplomatic tools. The legitimacy of these wars caused a heated debate between left-wing and right-wing opponents. During this period (except for a short and much-opposed term of the *Labor party*), Israel was ruled by the *Likud party*, which established a counter right-wing hegemony, composed of many *Mizrahim*. The differences between these two repertoires do not end with their reference points, but are also shown in the ways they portray the fallen soldiers. The *Ashkenazi* songs characterise the soldier as an un-marked, "universal" human being, who at the same time has the characteristics of the *Sabra*: committed, brave, strong, and willing to devote his life to the collective. For example, in the song *"We're from the same village,"* the soldier who speaks to the audience remains anonymous. We do not know his first name, only his "last name" – an Israeli from the village. This Israeli is speaking in the name of an imagined togetherness, of a collective that shares with him the same biography and characteristics. Thus, the *Sabra* is represented as the only frame through which one can become an Israeli (soldier); An Israeli (soldier) can be nothing but a *Sabra*. The speaker in the song *"All we pray for"* is also anonymous and *Sabra* at the same time. His image and voice represent the image and voice of all the soldiers, as if this was the only local cultural model available in order to become an Israeli. The song "The middle of Tammuz" demonstrates the same phenomenon: all the soldiers represent the *Sabra*; the *Sabra* and them are perceived as one inseparable unit. In contrast, the *Mizrahi* songs do not emphasise the hegemonic characteristics of the soldiers but the private-personal aspects of their daily lives. The songs remember fondly sweet moments when the soldiers come back home after a long period of time in service, the intimate gestures between the soldier and his loving mom, and the cozy Shabbat dinner table shared by the soldier and his family. The songs also describe in detail the deep, all-embracing sadness that engulfs the mother when she loses her son, and the endless depression surrounding her life due to her loss. These emotional and personal aspects of grief and sorrow replace the *Ashkenazi* songs' emphasis on the soldiers' national characters, features, and self-sacrifice. *Kedma's* hybrid musical program thus reflects the tension between the different periods and hegemonies, but also the different ways the hegemony and the counter-hegemony are imagined together through this musical program. Thus, the ceremony's composition highlights two main points of divergence and complementation. The first refers to the ways the soldiers are represented, and the second refers to the war time-zones they represent. While the songs from the "heroic period" characterise the soldier by the hegemonic *Ashkenazi Sabra* features, songs from the "controversial period" characterise the soldier by a model that does not correspond to that of the *Sabra*. Furthermore, in the songs from the "heroic period" the particular image of the *Sabra* soldier symbolises the collective aspects of war. In the songs from the "controversial period" the universal image of the Israeli soldier symbolises the particular-emotional aspects of war. What does this hybrid musical juxtaposition tell us and what type of nationhood can be read from it? In the case of the *Kedma* ceremony, viewing these integrative representations as a kind of negotiation, which according to Geertz' (1973) can even turn the ritual site into a setting of conflict and division, exposed a "nationhood" that deflected from that of the traditional ceremonies. In the process of collective identity formation, the school's choice embedded feelings of belonging through performances that expressed different images/periods. These choices created an experience that deviated from the traditional performance but challenged neither the discourse of nationhood nor the process of nation building. In other words, the fact that the ceremony was not coherent did not imply that we can read from it an anti-national discourse. On the contrary, the non-coherent national aspects that are represented in the ceremony suggest that a different national culture/

community is coming into being. This national culture/community is still committed, and does not intend to relinquish the cultural corner-stones of the ceremony and the nation. At the same time, this national culture/community is producing new cultural materials, for example: Arab-style music that expresses patriotic narratives. These materials do not aim to imply sub-cultural claims, nor do these materials aim to imply that the nation should recreate itself in a multicultural fashion. These materials are loyal to the invented tradition of the hegemonic ceremony and to the notion of one united society standing against the Arab world/threat. The mix of the *Ashkenazi* and *Mizrahi* cultures in the ceremony, thus, should be perceived as a site where national cul-ture is changing, but not challenging the national ideology. In the last decade the Israeli society has witnessed a few attempts that strived to widen the "community of suffering." One of them was the *Kedma Tel Aviv* school's ceremony on Holocaust Memorial Day. The school's staff decided to light a memorial candle dedicated to the non-Jewish victims of the holocaust, among them: homosexuals and lesbians, communists, anarchists, and disabled people. This ceremony was pub-licly criticised and condemned, claiming that the school was decrying both the victims and the nation (Barkay and Levy, 1999). There are even claims that the school was closed due to the controversy that the ceremony caused (Karpel, 2014). Even though the changes the *Kedma* ceremony implemented – referring to controversial wars, incorporat-ing Arab-style music, portraying a non-*Sabra* image of the soldier, and paying attention to personal aspects of mourning – are not minor, they still exist side by side with the hegemonic features of the ceremony. Hence, this move can be viewed not as a cultural opposition to the ethnic hierarchy, but as the cultural ramification of the ethnic hierar-chy. The ethnic hierarchy served as a way to create one culture for one nation, but as the *Kedma* ceremony reflects, the ethnic hierarchy ended up creating ways to widen the cultural borders of the nation. The *Kedma* ceremony's hybridity demonstrates one possible way to widen the cultural borders, instead of drawing borders. Thus, an ethnicity that was marked by the hegemonic national culture as a problem is now returning as a solution, loaded with much more bargaining power. The *HaTikva* national anthem, which ended the ceremony at *Kedma,* merged the performance, once again, with the collectivised narrative. This part that closed the ceremony, as well as the part that started it, are shared by all Jewish Israelis. "Maybe, someday," Says Avi, "What is now understood by some people as 'authenticity' [...] will be accept-able in the future as Israeli."

10 The IDF recruiting program

Focusing on the school's position with regards to nationality cannot be completed without paying attention to the ways the students dealt with enlistment to the IDF. Serving in the IDF at the age of 18 is compulsory for all Israeli Jews, both men and women, and for some of the Druze, Circassians, and Bedouins. The only ones not subject to mandatory recruitment are Palestinians living in Israel, Jewish yeshiva students and orthodox women, and those declaring themselves pacifists. Disabled people are also exempt from military service, but they are given the option of volunteering. Young people who have been found fit for recruitment but choose not to enlist face legal procedures. The period of service stands at 30 months for men and 18 months for women (Defence Service Law, 1986). The passage from high school to the military service is accompanied by various special educational programs that aim to prepare the students for their service. These programs are perceived as extracurricular and thus are not compulsory, even though they are approved by the Israeli Education Ministry and are usually included by all the public high schools throughout Israel (with the exception of Palestinian and ultra-orthodox schools) (Dahan-Kalev and Lebel, 2003). It is important to note that since serving in the army in Israel in mandatory, this type of militaristic socialisation extends throughout the Israeli education system, as opposed, for example, to the U.S.A., where this type of military socialisation is directed mostly to the lower classes, students of color, and students at risk, in order to replace racial with national identification (Bartlett and Lutz, 1998). The programs' goals are to encourage the students to serve, and to increase volunteering for IDF combat units. The programs also seek to prepare the students for the recruitment process, which starts when they are about to finish high school. The social agents that conduct these programs are young male and female Israeli soldiers (usually Jewish) that serve in various units and in different roles, among them combat fighters. Sometimes, high schools ask that the lectures be conducted by soldiers that graduated from their own institutions. The lecture is given in school during the students' last year of study, when they reach the 12th grade. The meeting enables the soldiers-instructors to give out information regarding the service and the different units and roles available for the soldiers to-be. The soldiers-instructors also share with the students their personal experiences from their own service, in order to personalise the process and increase the students' motivation to serve. The students are welcomed to participate in the lecture by adding comments and asking questions. It is important to note that besides the military, there are various companies in the private and civil sector that also offer similar services (Levy et al., 2007). Thus, education for military service has been accused of reproducing ethnic-class differentiations and hierarchies (Levy and Sasson-Levy, 2008).

As a major socialisation agency, the school is recruited to the state's/military's efforts to encourage students to enlist in combat units through yet more channels. The cultural work that preserves the powerful symbol of the soldier is carried out by hosting retired high-ranking military officers who share personal stories about famous combats/wars in which they played important roles; Visiting base camps and participating in basic military training and even practice shooting; Travelling to famous battle sites and monuments for the fallen soldiers during the annual school trip; And exploring military museums dedicated to different army corps. These efforts have even increased these days, since there is a decline in the motivation to serve in combat units. The decline – from 71% that sought to enlist in combat roles in 2016 to 69% in the following year – is attributed to the preference of the new recruits to serve in what they call "a meaningful service" (technological units and cyber defense). These units have higher exchange-value in the job market and thus are perceived as offering a more beneficial service (Yehoshua, 2017). But despite this previous decline in volunteering, the army managed to recruit the required number of soldiers to serve in combat roles, due to the military's efforts in schools (ibid). These efforts are part of a wider phenomenon that shapes the Israeli culture in line with the military's principles. This phenomenon was called by Kimmerling (1993) the "militaristic culture." The militaristic culture aims to influence all walks of daily life in line with the goals, interests, discourses, and narrative of the military. Thus, the militaristic culture can be traced not only in shared beliefs and values, but also in the ways the economy, the job marked, the division of social goods, and the political system are shaped in accordance with the militaristic principles. Since September 2011, this tendency has gained a lot of power, both in the global political arena and in the public view, which has led to the justification of armed conflicts, violence, and killings (Lutz, 2002).

Due to Israel's militaristic culture, serving in combat units is hence perceived as an important civic duty. This duty is represented as crucial for the security of Israeli residents and for the existence and stability of the state. This duty is also considered as crucial due to the common notion that Israel is surrounded by a hostile Arab world ("A few against many"), and due to the ongoing open-ended relentless war, especially with *Hamas*. Furthermore, the call to serve is directed to all the Israeli Jewish citizens, and thus is perceived as a unifying civic duty and discourse that overcomes ethnic and class divides ("the people's army") (Ben-Eliezer, 1995). In this light, the IDF has also been perceived as a "melting pot," where soldiers from different backgrounds can meet and thus blur social and cultural differences and boundaries (Swirski, 1999). However, despite being perceived as a social equaliser, the army service, at the same time, mediates and modifies the citizenship status of the civilian-soldiers in accordance with their military service (Burk, 1995; Tilly, 1996). This republican discourse/ethos, which highlights the "common good," draws a line between the mode and track of service and civil rights, privileges, and social status, thus contributing to the multilayered citizenship system that has evolved in Israel (Shafir and Peled, 2002). Hence, the connection between citizenship, social status, and military service is two-folded. It is not just that the military service predicts the status of citizenship, but the status of citizenship also predicts the mode of the military service. In other words, ethnicity and class play a crucial role in the process of enrollment in the army and attainment of high-status roles during service. As in other armies, the IDF military system is stratified along ethnic, race, and class lines (Enloe, 1980). This stratification has created notable differences between tracks, ranks, and roles. Thus, while the elite combat units are mostly composed of middle-class *Ashkenazi* soldiers that benefit from this position after finishing their service, the "blue color" units are mostly composed of low-class *Mizrahi* soldiers and immigrants from the former USSR (Levy, 2006). This division of labor is partly based on an "ethnic map" which demarcates groups according to their psychological, cognitive, and behavioral ability, by using various mechanisms of tracking (Mizrachi, 2004). How did the students respond to the military service, and the national notions embedded in it, during their experience in the IDF program? How did ethnicity and class shape their responses to the IDF's call for combat service?

The students were enthusiastic when they first saw the soldiers enter the school gates. It was in the middle of the day, after they had studied intensively for the upcoming matriculation exams. After the recess ended, they all gathered in the classroom and started the meeting with the army's representatives, which lasted two hours. Although the previous class, led by the English teacher, had been attended by only six students, in the course of the meeting with the army representatives the class became almost totally full. The army's representatives – a young female and a young male soldier – served in a combat unit. The soldiers' appearance fitted the national image of the *Sabra* combat fighter: the soldiers were carrying weapons, speaking in a tough language and tone, and using only the masculine gender while talking. The meeting started with the soldiers' story about their personal recruitment process and the way they experienced it. The class was in silence. All the students listened to the story attentively. After the soldiers finished their personal story, they asked the students about their forthcoming enlistment. When this question was raised regarding the students' future service, the discussion took the shape of a struggle. Itzik, a male student, said:

> I have problems at home, my mom is a single mother, I work as a porter and a cleaner to help her, I have to serve close to home [...] I can't afford to hang around doing all kind of things. I'm needed, I'm really needed, much needed at home.
>
> Markovich (2012, p. 188)

Dudu, another male student, said: "There's no way I'm leaving home, I have to help out at home because my father is disabled (Markovich, 2012, p. 189)." And Emi, a male student, added: "We can't leave home and disappear for weeks [...] no. we have to give a hand at home, help the parents." The students' first responses to the general question that was directed toward them by the soldiers exposed their defensive position. Even though the soldiers did not confront the students directly with the issue of volunteering for combat units, the students were replying to this "hidden" question/narrative. All the students that responded in this part of the meeting were males, due to the normative masculine assumption that demands national and military self-sacrifice first from the man. The students' responses demonstrated an apologetic manner, which was accompanied with different reasons and circumstances: "my mom is a single mother," "my father is disabled," "help the parents." This symbolic social-geographical location was further emphasised by Moti, a male student:

> I will not serve in any combat unit. I mean [...] I will not, I'm not going to do that, being far away from home, from the neighbor-hood, for a long time. Come on guys (referring to the soldiers), leave us alone (a slang expression meaning "don't bother us").
> Dudu, a male student, added to Moti's words, "It's not the kind of thing the guys here do."

These stances, which emphasised the "home" and the "neighbor-hood," can be positioned in the opposite pole to the self-sufficient combat unit soldiers' locations, which are placed, geographically and mentally, in remote and rather "autonomous" training areas far away from home. The students' responses echo the responses of low-class *Mizrahi* juveniles that finished their mandatory service and explained their enrollment in "blue color" roles citing their commitment to their family's needs (Tabib-Calif, 2015). But what do the students' positions/locations reveal about their ideological position/location? It seems that the students' limited choices, driven by their personal, social, and economic status, do not stem from their national standpoint. The students did not object to the army service or the patriotic mentality that is embedded in the army service (especially in combat units). Further-more, the students did not dismiss, by any mean, their obligation to the nation. But despite having no objection to the national-patriotic feelings and roles, they did not identify with the combat soldiers in general, and with those standing in front of them in particular. The students rather identified with a different collective – "the neigh-borhood" and "the guys." In other words, even though the students demonstrated their loyalty to the nation by being willing to serve, they presented a different narrative of service. Not a different attitude, but different circumstances that rely on a different emotional knowl-edge of being needed at home. This standpoint marked the army not just as a national space but also as a space that is subordinated to a socio-ethnic-based hierarchy. Thus, while the army was characterised through the soldiers' responses as a rather fixed and stable space, the students' responses characterised the army as a space that is tailored differently to different social groups. The army's ideological basis was not questioned. The students did not doubt the patriotic notion embedded in the army service. As proof of that, they were willing to serve (rather than not serve at all), in servicing jobs: drivers, cooks, armorers, and so forth, despite the low status associated with men that are positioned in these tracks. Thus, the students doubted the part that the army can take in their lives, and the efforts that they can invest in the army service. It is important to note that the ethnic component – *Mizrahi* – was silenced in the students' remarks. The students mentioned the difficulty of their everyday life, which prevented them from taking part in a challenging service, without explicitly referring to ethnicity. This tendency was further stressed in the female student Mali's response:

> The combat soldier he [...] you (pointing to the male soldier) you can afford that. You don't have the pressures. The parents that need you. The home that always asks you to give a hand and help and think about your siblings.

Mali suggested that the soldiers that served in combat units "earned" their service, and thus glorification, through their privileged social position ("you don't have the pressures"). Like those who spoke before her, she also claimed that there are some a priori conditions that determine the *Kedma* students' future assignment's modes and tracks ("parents that need you," "give a hand and help"). But like the other students, she was also cautious, and avoided the ethnic signifier. Instead of using ethnicity, Mali preferred to use rather general words, like parents, home, and siblings. Without marking the ethnic positioning as a variable that evaluates and asserts social realities, the class positioning remained the only explanation to the standpoint toward the military service. After the students expressed themselves, the soldiers replied:

MALE SOLDIER: Anyone can succeed. The army is for everyone. The army gives everyone a chance. The opportunities are open for all. It doesn't matter who you are, it's up to you.

FEMALE SOLDIER: If each person pulls himself together and tells himself that he can achieve what he wants, and does the maximum, then it will happen, and from then on, the sky is the limit, he can succeed in anything in life.

Markovich (2012, p. 189)

The soldiers' responses caused confusion in the class even though the universalistic idea of "service for all" is common in the Israeli Zionist society (Levy and Sasson-Levy, 2008). From the soldiers' point of view, the army suggested a path for integration through an inclusive socialisation system that offers equal opportunities for all. This system, it was hinted, is indifferent to class and social position ("It doesn't matter who you are"), and at the same time celebrates the individuals' efforts and motivation ("it's up to you"). Thus, class or social position did not appear in the soldiers' discourse or in their (army) world. The soldiers' attitude is consistent with a widespread assumption that dodging military service is the defectors' fault. Thus, this act can result in various formal and informal sanctions because the performance of military service in Israel is tied to social rights in the areas of employment, qualification for a mortgage, entitlement for study grants, and so on (since most Palestinian living in Israel are exempt from military service in the IDF, and since alternative forms of national service have been rejected by most of the Palestinian leadership, Palestinian citizens suffer from the curtailment of their social rights). Ronen, a male student, who based his stance on his family member's experience, said emotionally in response: "My brother failed all the exams, he never had a chance because he comes from here (from the neighborhood) (Markovich, 2012, p. 189)." Ronen mentioned the exams (health tests, intelligence tests, psychological tests, and so forth), that those wishing to serve in elite units must go through. Some of these examinations are held before the military service, while the candidates are still in high school. By mentioning the exams, he was trying to draw attention to the nature of the military's induction process and thus to the congruence between the composition of the IDF combat and elite units, and the social stratification that characterises the world outside the army's gates. But like the other students, he avoided his ethnic background and did not refer to it explicitly ("because he comes from here"). This debate exposed the duality in which the students were caught. On the one hand they were welcomed to take part in the hegemonic units ("anyone can succeed," "the army is for everyone"). On the other hand, various social and economic factors prevented them from full participation. Thus, the students, like a large part of the marginalised groups in the Israeli society, were not able to fulfil the demands required by the national-military-masculinity norms (Levy, 2006). This position locked the students outside of the linear progress route that starts with being a "good student" and ends with demonstrating "good citizenship," due to various reasons that the students spoke about explicitly. But still, the ethnic signifiers were absent from the discussion. The students concealed the ethnic factor, and certainly did not make the ethnic boundaries visible. Even though ethnicity played a role in other events that clashed with nationality (as in the case of the annual school trip and the ceremony for the fallen soldiers), when meeting with the IDF combat soldiers, ethnicity was downgraded and placed outside of the discussion. This choice transformed the students' narrative from an ethnic-oriented narrative to a class-oriented narrative, suggesting that class is a more legitimate reason for not serving in combat units than ethnicity. By choosing class, the students also saved themselves from the impossible position of declaring that they were "nationally disabled" by their own (ethnic) identity. Thus, explanations that were anchored in economic personal problems were more "affordable" for them, considering the quasi-sacred place the military service occupies in the Israeli society. In other words, moving from ethnicity to class made the students' relinquishment more legitimate, and at the same time did not harm the "natural" alliance between the students and the soldiers or the consensus regarding the importance of the military service. In other words, the students were holding a position that can be described as militarism without full military participation. This unique situation deviates from the assumptions of postcolonial theory, which suggest that the "Other" is trapped in the desire to mimic the hegemony, and at the same time deconstruct the hegemony (Bhabha, 1990), since in this case it is neither mimicry nor deconstruction. As opposed to cases like the recruitment of black low-class students to combat units in the U.S.A, where students join these forces in order to use the military's "color blind" promise to advance their socio-economic mobility (Aguirre and Brooke, 2005), the *Kedma* students emphasised their socio-economic difficulties in order to customise their sense of belonging. This situation also deviates from post-Zionist claims that encourage *Mizrahim* to leave the nation building project, in which they are not accepted as equals, and develop utopian, bricolage, transgressive ideologies that will bridge between Orient and Occident (Chetrit, 2000). As part of the ethnonational collective, the students did not express any wish to form a new path for their identity construction. The students' choice accepted the national demands, even though they could not fully fulfill them. The opposite happened when the students were exposed to civic participation.

11 Education for civic engagement

"We do not do civic activities," declared one of the students at the beginning of the meeting with the representative of the students' council. The students' council held a meeting at the school in order to get the students acquainted with various programs of civic engagement in which they can enroll. These activities were presented to the students as part of the obligatory civic participation program held in Israeli public high schools. The program is called "personal obligation" ("מחויבות אישית"). It aims to address issues of public concern and give a hand in tackling them. The students can volunteer for various activities and with different target populations, among them: children with a physical or mental disability, underprivileged children, seniors, and injured animals. The activities take place in non-profit, non-governmental organisations, which operate in both the local and the national sphere: rehabilitation hospitals, after-school child care facilities, elderly homes, the "Society for the Prevention of Cruelty to Animals," the "Magen David Adom" organisation (Israeli equivalent of the "Red Cross" first aid organisation), and the "Fire Scouts." The "personal obligation" project is an initiative introduced by the Israeli Ministry of Education in 1979 (Director General's Communiqué, 2002). Participation in the project is obligatory during 10th grade. Those who do not take part in the program are not eligible to receive the matriculation certificate. Each student must complete 60 hours of volunteering per year, that is, two hours of volunteering each week.

This field of extracurricular civic education in Israel has changed over the years. When the program started, its goals were directed toward the burning social problems and their possible solutions. Today, the current goals focus on the students' educational, cognitive, and emotional development that is gained through participation in these out-of-school activities (Rubowitz, 2007).

Thus, research findings emphasise the program's impact on students, and specifically the different ways the programs grant the participants opportunity for experiential learning, enhance their ability to cope with the pressures of the maturation process, and increase their self-competence, leadership, and interpersonal skills (Almog, Shenhar and Flaisher, 2003). These findings frame the "personal obligation" program as, ostensibly, an all-encompassing phenomenon that imposes a linear developmental process. Only a handful of studies have differentiated between the students' ethnic identity-class position and the students' attitude to volunteering. Findings regarding the volunteers' backgrounds indicate that the typical participant in these programs is a female student who has parents that have gained higher education, and whose family tends to participate in civic activities (Cohen, Schmida and Ferman, 1985). Furthermore, it was found that due to their commitment to their communities, Palestinian students living in Israel were more interested in future civic activism in their community than their Jewish Israeli counterparts (Ichilov, 2004). These differences echo findings that indicate that there is a gap between the extracurricular opportunities that students from different backgrounds are exposed to, and thus between the students' potential civic participation (Lobman, 2011). Hence, the achievement gap between privileged and non-privileged students is also reproduced in their extracurricular involvement (Lutkus and Weiss, 2007). These gaps can lead to harsh differences in the mode and extent of the students' future democratic participation in line with their social positioning and class.

The democratic participation adventure started at *Kedma* when a young man – the representative of the city's student council – and a young man and woman – the representatives of a left-wing youth group that operates in Jerusalem – held a meeting with the students of the 9th and 10th grades. All the representatives were in their 20s. None of them were living in the neighborhood. They grew up, studied, and lived in the privileged parts of Jerusalem. The representatives started the meetings by changing the seating arrangements in class. Oren (male) and Rotem (female), the youth group leaders, held the meeting in the 9th grade. Immediately after they entered the classroom, they moved the teacher's table and shoved it to the corner. Instead of sitting behind the teacher's table, they took two deserted chairs that were thrown away in one of the class's empty spaces and sat on them. They were both sitting with their legs crossed, wearing the dark blue shirt – the formal uniform of the youth organisation. The other meeting, which was held with the 10th grade, was attended by only a few students. Even though they did not have big crowds, Oren and Rotem took the trouble to re-organise the seats in the shape of a semi-circle. In a different meeting that took place in the same classroom, Asaf (male) – the students' city council representative, chose to sit on the table of one of the students. From that stand point he conducted the conversation with the students. The atmosphere that the different representatives created goes hand in hand with the non-formal image that surrounds the out-of-school activities, and with the teenage rebellion image that accompanies them. At the same time, this atmosphere served as a platform that increased the students' attentiveness and emphasised a wishful symmetrical power relation between the various representatives and the students. In this "intimate" space that they created, the representatives began the conversation by presenting themselves and their role in the different organisations. After doing that, they proceeded with their personal engagement with the organisation, and the different paths that led them to deepen their relationships with these activities. Oren shared with the 10th grade students the harsh difficulties he suffered when he was about their age: "I was a very quiet person, like [...] really introvert." He then continued and told the students about the ways the activities in the youth group helped him to strengthen his self-image and to overcome his social fears: "It (the involvement with the youth group activities) built me as a person and gave me the confidence of who I am, and what I am capable of doing." Rotem also shared with the class memories from a few years back, when she started volunteering after long hesitations. She told the students about her lack of motivation and interest in extracurricular activities: "The activity in the youth group was nothing [...] it was... I went there only because other kids from my class go." Then she continued her story and revealed how this activity became, unexpectedly, her social mission, changing her self-perception as well as her whole outlook and worldview: "It (the activity) became something that I am [....] that I felt that because of it I managed to move things, to act, to change. I realised that this activity was helping me grow." In the meeting that was held in the 10th grade, Asaf told the students about his feeling disconnected throughout the years he spent in school: "I really did not find myself a place in class." And how, eventually, he found himself anew through the activity in the students' city council: "I did a lot of things for the school and for the community and found out things I did not know about myself." After the representatives finished sharing their personal engagement with the various activities, they explained to the students, in details, what are the organisations' goals and modes of operation. After doing that they turned to the "administrative" parts of the participation (the extent and scope of the volunteering activities they were expected to do), and then they invited the students to share their opinions regarding the activities/organisations and to ask questions. It is important to note that all these meetings were held without the teacher being involved. In some cases, the teacher left the class a few minutes after the meeting had begun. Being in class during the meetings highlighted the question regarding the terms that frame the evolution of a civically engaged student, and in particular, the ways through which a civically engaged student comes into being in disadvantaged contexts.

For the students *of Kedma*, to become civically engaged was to contribute to the nation. Even though the representatives tied up together various reasons and goals related to the activities they offered the students, "giving to the nation" was the students' focal point. "Giving to the nation" is not a unique characteristic of the students of *Kedma*. The republican discourse and the national emotions that accompany it are central to the Israeli Jewish society, and it certainly does not concern only underprivileged groups. The republican discourse is used in order to emphasise the important role of the Jewish national groups in the process of nation building, and in order to legitimise the benefits that they gain from their involvement (Peled, 2008). This notion, which is composed of national goals and civic virtues, underestimates the contribution of non-hegemonic ethnic Jewish groups, while completely denying the collective rights of the Palestinian citizens of Israel (Jamal, 2007; Jabareen and Agbaria, 2017). Moshe, one of the male students that attended the meeting with the youth group leaders, explained this Gordian knot that ties the nation and the civic engagements: "To give something from yourself to the nation is important because we have to be strong together against our enemies." Yifat, a female student that participated in the youth group leaders' meeting, had a similar claim: "contributing to the nation (is being done) so that we will all be stronger, all of us as a society." The words "strong," "together" and "all" recurred over and over in the students' comments. Emi, a male student, even described in detail the various ways in which one action (volunteering) can lead to the other (strengthening); in which the individual can contribute to the nation:

> If you can volunteer, let's say in the civil guard (a division in the "Police and Community" branch of the Israeli Police. Its manpower consists mainly of civilian volunteers), it can be very helpful for the country and the people. Or for example, if you volunteer in a hospital or something like that, it can also help. But this (volunteering in the hospital) is not so important in my opinion. The police force, and things like that, it (the volunteering) is

important to defend the state and in order to have a strong nation, because we (the Jewish population) are always under attack and we must always be ready, so that we don't fall.

Emi is measuring the individual's contribution to the nation in light of the nation's needs. The nation's needs are defined by him as those of the Jewish population. In other words, when the "common good" had greater relevance to the nation's security (civil guard) it was perceived as more important. However, when the "common good" had less relevance to the nation's security (hospital) it was perceived as less important. The students also claimed that not being active in defending the nation from its enemies is damaging both the individual and the nation. Rinat, a female student, articulated this notion by saying: "Those who do not contribute to the nation are in my view dodgers." And Yossi, a male student, added: "How can one not contribute (to the state). From my point of view, this (not contributing) is a crime in a nation like ours where you always have to fight for your life." Amir, a male student, explained these ideas in detail:

When you do not engage in civic participation, then you see what comes out of it (not engaging) for us. All those who are not doing anything, instead of contributing to the nation, are just being a burden. They just take for themselves. They do not understand that without giving to the nation we won't have anything in this country. It wouldn't be good for them (those who do not give to the nation) also. Those people are a shame. They are ruining it for themselves and for us.

Civic activities that were not attached to defense, such as volunteering in underprivileged students' clubs or with disabled people, were perceived by the students as volunteering for "society." As opposed to volunteering for the nation, this kind of "giving" was accepted with much less enthusiasm. Some students expressed indifference toward these activities: "It is boring," (Shoshi, female student), while other students said: "It's not interesting for me" (David, male student). Some students wondered why they should invest their efforts in these fields: "I don't understand why I would even be asked to do things like that" (Ari, male student), and others commented: "It (these activities) doesn't interest me" (Esther, female student). When the representatives insisted that contributing to society also meant contributing to the nation, the students dismissed these claims by putting this conclusion in context:

ANAT (FEMALE STUDENT): I don't feel like wanting to participate in those activities.

OREN: But it also helps the nation. The society constructs the nation, doesn't it?

In response, the students sketched, yet again, the boundaries between the society and the nation by positioning their identity in the national context:

ADEL (FEMALE STUDENT): Why do I have to do stuff like that?

ROTEM: It is part of the citizen's obligations toward society.

OVED (MALE STUDENT): I think you are confusing us with someone else. What will we gain in return for this?

Adel hinted that others were volunteering, in what was coined by the students as "society." Oved's "joke" added to Adel's words, that for him and for his community ("us"), the key to participation is not anchored in society but elsewhere. In other words, volunteering in society was not profitable enough ("What will we gain in return for this?"). This remark emphasised not just the importance of the nation, but also the rewards given to those who contribute to the nation. Furthermore, this remark claimed that different civic engagements hold different values for different people. This web, composed of nationality, civic culture, and power, exposes the acts of civic participation as a stratified field. In this field, citizenship is granted to residents of all ethnic-class groups, but the benefits of civic participation are not granted and distributed in the same manner to all ethnic-class groups. "Giving to the nation," thus, holds symbolic power that is much more important to some groups than "giving to society." The split that the students drew between nation and society can be seen, at first glance, as rather dichotomous. Oz, a male student, explained this by way of negation: "Let those from *Meretz* (Meretz, vigor in Hebrew, is a left-wing, social-democratic, and green party that is most identified with middle-class *Ashkenazi* voters) volunteer in those clubs." Oz is implying that in the Israeli society those who are involved in civic engagements in "society" are the privileged ones. Data regarding the voluntary sector's characteristics indicate that Oz's assumption is correct. The *Ashkenazi* group not only constitutes one of the dominant volunteering groups in Israel (Haski-Leventhal, Yogev-Keren and Katz, 2011), but also transforms this investment into social profit that promotes their structural privileges and authority in shaping the volunteering field (Shachar, 2013). Thus, not to invest in the hegemonic practices connected to the nation was perceived as an advantage that one group (those from *Meretz*) has over the others. In this manner, participating in civic engagements that are perceived as less valuable can be afforded only by the hegemonic groups. The hegemonic groups have nothing to lose by not manifesting the hegemonic practices, since they do not have to prove or fight for their social status. The social status of this group (coined by the students as *Meretz*) is given to them in advance, not in light of their current contribution, but due to their social category's position in the nation. But for the representatives, the politics of political involvement has nothing to do with ethnicity or class: "How is *Meretz* connected to this?" asked Rotem. From her point of view, there is no one version of participation: "I don't choose. To act only in this kind of activity and not in other kinds is sometimes not to act." Rotem does not accept the students' decisive choices and even hints that dismissing a whole sector of civic participation turns the students' engagements into "semi-voluntarism." Being blind to the power relations that are woven into the students' experiences, as well as to one's own advantage, characterises the educational system's policy as well.

Various attempts to force belonging by civic participation, of both Palestinian students living in Israel and ultra-orthodox *Haredi* groups, are taking place (Agbaria, Mustafa and Jabareen, 2015). Some of these attempts are generating alternatives to civic participation that are based on a religiously-inspired worldview, such as *ZAKA* ("Disaster Victim Identification"), which aids in the identification of the victims of terrorism and road accidents and gathers body parts and spilled blood for proper Jewish burial, and *Yad Sarah,* which provides free loans of medical and rehabilitative home-care equipment (Stadler, Lomsky-Feder and Ben-Ari, 2008; Vardi, Orr and Finkelstein, 2019). Others preserve the Jewish Zionist hegemony. Zionist Jewish marginalised groups, as opposed to these groups, do not have to generate new concepts of participation but to "estimate" the different values that they gain from participating in the available channels. The discrepancies, generated by the clash between ethnic, class, and national positioning, thus expose the commodified nature of participation and belonging, especially the channels through which participation is being determined and belonging is being earned. Hence, civic engagements that center on values of justice, equality, and pluralism are postponed in the name of national discourse and values. Being aware of the ethnic-class divisions, the students retain their status by sticking to the non-universalised modes of volunteering, which still serve as the ultimate path for belonging to the Israeli society.

12 Concluding remarks

The new sociology of education, which relies on critical assumptions, tends to sketch reality through macro social and political power relations. These efforts strive to track the ways the social-cultural hegemony develops and establishes binary social structures, which are subordinated to depoliticised and naturalised systems and mechanisms of stratification and control. As opposed to these top-down structural models, the current analysis follows the dynamics of teachers, students, and parents in one national school, which serves an underprivileged ethnic-class group by using the toolkit of critical pedagogy. Grounded in everyday organised and spontaneous events in school, this interpretive empirical study tried to track the process of both identity construction and educational outcomes, and the way they have been carved by the school and the students through various ideological and institutionalised forces. Despite the emancipating aspirations of *Kedma*, delving into the school's everyday life exposed a complex social reality that juxtaposed class, ethnicity, nationality, and critical pedagogy, in a way that was not always in line with the school's desires. Thus, more than the research unveiled the triumph gained by using critical discourse and praxis, or the successful production of a "consciousness shift," it exemplified the ideological and structural conditions that the school and the students experienced, and the different ways they coped with the educational demands. In this process of establishing their identity and their educational achievements, the role of non-cognitive aspects of learning was highlighted. Maneuvering their way through an ideologically patterned curriculum, critical pedagogy, civic ceremonies, extracurricular activities, and the formal matriculation exams, the students represented, modified, and sometimes reproduced their identity as well as the mode and extent of their "educability," in light of the national culture/identity. The national culture/identity was one of the main components that determined the school's life. Nationality was one of the most important dimensions/aspects of the disadvantage identity, and thus the dimension/aspect that actively constructed the relationship between disadvantagedness and educational success. Literature on nationality and education stresses two main perspectives regarding the ways marginalised students cope with the hegemonic nationality. One way to approach hegemonic nationality is to adopt a compliant-functional approach that is expressed through pragmatic acceptance of the nation. The other way is to adopt a harsh resistance to nationality, which is expressed through hostility and rejection of the nation. Thus, this dichotomous divide further establishes the marginal group as the nation's antagonist. The less dichotomous approach performed by the *Kedma* students exposed the relations with nationality as a combination of various frames, including ethnicity, class, and critical pedagogy, creating new definitions of being national and being a student in a nationalised education system/society. Neither being pragmatists nor resisting, the school and the students and parents took part in a non-consistent process of identity formation that fluctuated between different aspects of their ethnic-class-national-critical position that occurred in different circumstances. On issues centered on their daily school life, the students sometimes chose to highlight their patriotic nationalism and even reclaim patriotism, on other occasions they emphasised their ethnic culture, on other occasions they expressed limitations forced on them due to their class position, and on other occasions they expressed their critical thinking. These conceptualisations were deployed differently in different contexts and represented the different purposes. Hence, these multiple, and even contradicting, positions, need to be understood as ideologically formed and legitimised within the web of power relations in which the school and the students were caught. These socio-political frames were not founded on a solid position, but rather on a position that exposed the idea of educational transformation as a dialectical and debatable process. Even though the teachers, students, and parents were part of a systematic critical socialisation process, this route did not necessarily lead to a systematic ideological change. The all-embracing critical identity/culture in which the teachers, students, and parents were embedded was sometimes replaced by different ethnic-class-national discourses and positions. In certain events, ethnicity and class framed the teachers', students', and parents' approach. This happened when ethnic-class positioning left them no choice but to choose to participate in the national matriculation exams rather than in the critical path of learning. In other cases, the ethnic-class positioning was stronger than the students' educational success in determining their self-perception and image. In other events, ethnicity and class were silenced by the students. This happened when the students refused to use their ethnic-class origin in a reflective critical way in the art class. But in other cases, it was ethnicity and class that dominated the situation. This happened on the annual school trip and during Remembrance Day for the Fallen Soldiers. In both cases the students negated the national culture and replaced it with their ethnic-class habits and customs. But yet in other cases, such as during the recruiting program with the military representatives, the students emphasized their class positioning and ignored their ethnic-class identity/positioning. Or highlighted nationality and dismissed society, as in the case of the extracurricular civic activity. What shaped the conditions under which these positions and strategies took place? Why did the school and the students choose to use ethnicity sometimes as a shield, sometimes as an "alibi," and sometimes as a non-existing characteristic? In all these junctions, nationality played a critical role. In other words, the teachers', students', and parents' choices always considered nationality and never relinquished the shared national identity. Hence, grappling with nationality formulated different approaches to ethnicity, class, and criticality, establishing a non-comprehensive identity/culture that was reflecting/widening the boundaries of the national discourse. Yet in all cases, the teachers, students, and parents were trying to reach a "cultural balance," one that embraced the national, the ethnic-class, and even the critical perspective, and nevertheless did not justify any anti-national discourse. Thus, each choice is awarded a national meaning, even when nationality was bypassed by the other dimensions of the school's identity/culture. In other words, the national notions were stronger than the other components of the school's identity/culture despite the national's marginalising power.

Moving beyond *Kedma's* case study thus raises the question of whether underprivileged groups can gain educational autonomy within a dominant national cultural identity. The centrality of the national ideology and the important role it fulfills in shaping and defining the identity of the modern citizen cannot be overestimated. Neo-liberalism is offering different ethnic groups various modes of assimilation that will enable the nation to "digest" them within the national borders. The New Right movement is offering them the option of "cultural fundamentalism," which emphasises the authentic characters of different ethnic groups and marginalises them on the basis of these differences (Spektorowski, 2000). The continuing relevance of national models of citizenship and belonging to various ethnic-class groups has not declined, even during post-national-globalised shifts

(Koopmans and Statham, 1999). In Israel, nationality is also subjected to powerful forces of change by neo-Zionist and post-Zionist tendencies. These poles – the religious particularistic and the civic universalistic – exemplify the breaking-up of the dominant nationalist ethos of Zionism (Ram, 2000). This trend allows the existence of a variety of sub-identities (such as: Palestinians living in Israel, Jewish-Arabs, modern-Orthodox), that strive to transform Israel's collective identity by lessening the dominance of the old national hegemony. But despite these efforts, the result is being accused of constructing either a "controlled multiculturalism" that permits the existence of identities that do not negate the national identity (Al-Haj, 2002), or a "supervised multiculturalism" that undermines the values of non-Zionist groups (Abu Asbah, 2018). It seems that the national ideology/culture is still the most relevant ideological platformer bridging ethnicity, class, and critical perspectives. In this atmosphere, the category of the Arab-Jews did not have much chance of overtaking nationality. The Arab-Jewis started the journey of the *Kedma* school by putting a bold mirror in front of the national hegemony's face. But, along the way, they turned into Jews that ethnicised their social-cultural relations with the nation only when this act did not limit their national inclusion or jeopardise the Zionist borders. Challenging the national worldview is thus an option that is yet to come.

References

Abu Asbah, K. (2018). Education for multiculturalism among Arab youth in Israel. *Diaspora, Indigenous, and Minority Education, 12*(1), 1–13.

Abu-Saad, I. (2006). Palestinian education in Israel: The legacy of the military government. *Holy Land Studies: A Multidisciplinary Journal, 5*(1), 21–56.

Addi-Raccah, A., & Ayalon, H. (2008). From high school to higher education: Curricular policy and postsecondary enrollment in Israel. *Educational Evaluation and Policy Analysis, 30*(1), 31–50.

Agbaria, A., Mustafa, M., & Jabareen, Y. (2015). 'In your face' democracy: Education for belonging and its challenges in Israel. *British Educational Research Journal, 41*(1), 143–175.

Aguirre, A. Jr., & Brooke, J. (2005). Militarizing youth in public education: Observations from a military-style charter school. *Social Justice, 32*(3), 148–162.

Al-Haj, M. (1995). *Education, Empowerment, and Control: The Case of the Arabs in Israel.* Albany, NY: SUNY Press.

Al-Haj, M. (2002). Multiculturalism in deeply divided societies: The Israeli case study. *International Journal of Intercultural Relations, 26*(2), 169–183.

Alcalay, A. (1987). The Sephardim and the 'Orientalization' of Israel. *Journal of Palestine Studies, 16*(4), 156–165.

Alkalay, A. (1993). *After Jews and Arabs: Remaking Levantine Culture.* Minneapolis: University of Minnesota Press.

Almog, I., Shenhar, M., & Flaisher, N. (2003). *The Influences of the Volunteering Educational Programs on its Participants.* Jerusalem: The Ministry of Education and Carmel institute for Social Research. [In Hebrew].

Almog, O. (2000). *The Sabra – The Creation of a New Jew.* Berkley: University of California Press.

Almog, O. (2004). *Farewell to Srulik.* Haifa: University of Haifa Press. [In Hebrew].

Amara, M., Azaiza, F., Hertz-Lazarowitz, R., & Mor-Sommerfeld, A. (2009). A new bilingual education in the conflict-ridden Israeli reality: Language practices. *Language and Education, 23*(1), 15–35.

Anderson, B. (2006). *Imagined Communities: Reflections on the Origin and Spread of Nationalism*. London: Verso.

Arar, K.H. (2015). Leadership for equity and social justice in Arab and Jewish schools in Israel: Leadership trajectories and pedagogical praxis. *International Journal of Multicultural Education, 17*(1), 162–187.

Avieli, N. (2013). Grilled nationalism: Power, masculinity, and space in Israeli barbeques. *Food, Culture and Society, 16*(2), 301–320.

Avissar, N. (2019). *Learning from the East: Mizrahi Culture, Education, and Tikun Olam*. Tel Aviv: Mofet Institute. [In Hebrew].

Ayalon, A. (2007). A model for teachers mentoring of poor and minority children: A case study of an urban Israeli school mentoring. *Mentoring and Tutoring, 15*(1), 5–23.

Ayalon, H., & Shavit, Y. (2004). Educational reforms and inequalities in Israel: The MMI hypothesis revisited. *Sociology of Education, 77*(2), 103–120.

Azaryahu, M. (1996a). The power of commemorative street names. *Society and Space, 14*(3), 311–330.

Azaryahu, M. (1996b). Mount Herzl: The creation of Israel's national cemetery. *Israel Studies, 1*(2), 46–74.

Bairey, Ben-Ishay, A. (1998). *Teacher Burnout and Consciousness Complexity: An Analysis of the Mentors at Kedma (An Alternative Israeli Highschool)* (Doctoral dissertation). Harvard University, Cambridge, MA.

Balibar, E., & Wallerstein, I. (1991). *Race, Nation, Class: Ambiguous Identities*. London: Verso.

Banks, J.A., & McGee Banks, C.A. (2010) (Ed.). *Multicultural Education, Issues and Perspectives*. Hoboken, NJ: Wiley.Bar-Gal, Y. (1993). *Moledet and Geography in Hundred Years of Zionist Education*. Tel Aviv: Am Oved. [In Hebrew].

Bar Shalom, Y., & Krumer-Nevo, M. (2007). The usage of qualitative research methods as means to empower disadvantaged groups: The example of the Kedma School in Jerusalem. *The International Journal of Interdisciplinary Social Sciences, 2*(1), 237–244.

Barkay, T., & Levy, G. (1999). Kedma School. *News from Within, XV*(6), 26–32.

Bartlett, L., & Lutz, C. (1998). Disciplining social differences: Some cultural politic of military training in public high school. *The Urban Review, 30*(2), 119–136.

Barur, Ben-David, O. (1998). Culture and nature in the trips conducted by the society for the protection of nature. In O. Abuhav, E. Hertzog, H.E. Goldberg & M. Emanuel (Eds.) *Israel: Local Anthropology, Studies in the Anthropology of Israel* (pp. 451–482). Tel Aviv: Tcherikover. [In Hebrew].

Bashi, J. (1983). *A Report on Kiryat-Malachi and Sderot*. Jerusalem: Van Leer Institute. [In Hebrew].

Ben-Amos, A. (2003). War commemoration and the formation of Israeli national identity. *Journal of Political and Military Sociology, 31*(2), 171–195.

Ben-Amos, A., & Bet-El, E. (1999). Holocaust Day and Memorial Day in Israeli schools: Ceremonies, education and history. *Israel Studies, 4*(1), 258–284.

Ben-Eliezer, U. (1995). A nation in arms: State, nation and militarism in Israel's first years. *Comparative Studies in Society and History, 37*(2), 264–285.

Ben Zvi, T. (2004). Mother tongue. In Y. Nizri (Ed.) *Eastern Appearance/ Mother Tongue: A Present that Stirs in the Thickets of Its Arab Past* (pp. 1–16). Tel Aviv: Babel.

Bekerman, Z. (2009). Israel: Unsuccessful and limited multicultural education. *South African Journal of Education, 6*(2), 132–145.

Bernstein, D., & Swirski, S. (1982). The rapid economic development of Israel and the emergence of ethnic division of labor. *British Journal of Sociology, 33*(1), 64–85.

Bhabha, K.H. (1990). The other question: Difference, discrimination and the discourse of colonialism. In R. Ferguson, M. Gever, T. Minhha & C. West (Eds.) *Out There: Marginalization and Contemporary Cultures* (pp. 71–87). Cambridge: MIT Press.

Billig, M. (1995). *Banal Nationalism.* London: Sage Publishing House.

Bilu, Y., & Witztum, E. (2000). War-related loss and suffering in Israeli society: A historical perspective. *Israel Studies, 5*(2), 1–32.

Bourdieu, P. (1984). *Distinction: A Social Critique of the Taste.* Cambridge, MA: Harvard University Press.

Bourdieu, P. (1993). *The Field of Cultural Production.* Cambridge: Polity Press.

Boyarin, D. (1997). *Unheroic Conduct: The Rise of Heterosexuality and the Invention of the Jewish Man.* Berkeley: University of California Press.

Bradley, W. (1992). History and the fine art cartel: The north/south inevitability. In P.M. Amburgy, D. Soucy, M. Stankiewicz, B. Wilson & M. Wilson (Eds.) *The History of Art Education* (pp. 234–240). Reston, VA: The National Art Education Association.

Burk, J. (1995). Citizenship status and military service: The quest for inclusion by minorities and conscientious objectors. *Armed Forces and Society, 21*(4), 503–529.

Carter, P. (1999). "Black" cultural capital, status positioning, and schooling conflicts for low-Income African American youth. *Social Problems, 50*(1), 136–155.

Carter, P. (2003). "Black" cultural capital, status positioning, and schooling conflicts for low-income African American youth. *Social Problems, 50*(1), 136–155.

Chalmers, G. (1999). Cultural colonialism and art education: Eurocentric and racist roots of art education. In D. Boughton & R. Mason (Eds.) *Beyond Multicultural Art Education: International Perspectives* (pp. 173–188). New York, NY: Waxmann Munster.

Chetrit, S.S. (1999). *The Ashkenazi Revolution is Dead.* Tel Aviv: Bimat kedem. [In Hebrew].

Chetrit, S.S. (2000). Mizrahi politics in Israel: Between integration and alternative. *Journal of Palestinian Studies, 29*(4), 51–65.

Chetrit, S.S. (2010). *Intra-Jewish Conflict in Israel: White Jews, Black Jews.* London and New York, NY: Routledge.

Coenders, M., & Scheepers, P. (2003). The effect of education on nationalism and ethnic exclusion: An international comparison. *Political Psychology, 24*(2), 313–343.

Cohen, D. (1991). *Contemplation and Experience in Music Education.* Jerusalem: The Magnes Press. [In Hebrew].

Cohen, M., Schmida, M., & Ferman, I. (1985). The personal involvement project: Differences between volunteering and non-volunteering high school pupils. *Megamot, 29*(2), 216–222. [In Hebrew].

Cohen, Y., Lewin-Epstein, N., & Lazarus, A. (2019). Mizrahi-Ashkenazi educational gaps in the third generation. *Research in Social Stratification and Mobility, 59*(February), 25–33.

Dahaf. (2000). *Pupils and Parents Opinions on Kedma High School.* Herzliya: Self-Publication. [In Hebrew].

Dahan, M., Eyal, D., Mironychev, N., & Shye, S. (2003). Have the gaps in education narrowed? On factors determining eligibility for the Israeli matriculation certificate. *Israel Economic Review, 1*(2), 37–69.

Dahan, Y. (2011). Privatization, school choice and educational equality. *Law and Ethics of Human Rights, 5*(2), 308–334.

Dahan, Y., & Levy, G. (2000). Multicultural education in the Zionist state – The Mizrahi challenge. *Studies in Philosophy and Education, 19*(5–6), 423–444.

Dahan-Kalev, H., & Lebel, U. (2003). Generals in school: On the growing connection between military and education. *Politics, 11–12*, 177–179. [In Hebrew].

Darder, A., Baltodano, M., & Torres, R.D. (Eds.). (2002). *The Critical Pedagogy Reader.* London and New York, NY: Routledge/Falmer.

Dattel, I. (2018). Israel's high school matriculation exams is big business, but do students benefit? *Haaretz,* 7.8.2018, pp. 26–28.

Defence Service Law. (1986). *Defence Service Law - Consolidated Version 5746-1986.* 30 Jan 1986. The State of Israel: Constitution, Legislation and Justice Committee of the Knesset.

Delpit, L. (1998). The silenced dialogue: Power and pedagogy in educating other people's children. *Harvard Educational Review, 58*(3), 280–298.

Director General's Communiqué. (2002). *Social and Non-Formal Education.* Jerusalem: The Ministry of Education. [In Hebrew].

Director General's Communiqué. (2005). *School Trips and Extracurricular Activities.* Jerusalem: The Ministry of Education. [In Hebrew].

Dolev, A. (1976). The Katamonim curse. *Maariv,* 9.6.1976. [In Hebrew].

Downey, D.B., Von Hippel, P.T., & Broh, B. (2004). Are schools the great equalizer? Cognitive inequality during the summer months and the school year. *American Sociological Review, 69*(5), 613–635.

Eliade, M. (1963). *Myth and Reality.* New York, NY: Harper and Row.

Enloe, C. (1980). *Ethnic Soldiers: State Security in Divided Societies.* Athens: Georgia University Press.

Entwisle, D.R., Alexander, K.L., & Olson, L.S. (1997). *Children, Schools, and Inequality.* Boulder, CO: Westview Press.

Erev Rav. (2011). Emergency conference dealing with the state of art teaching in Israeli schools. *Erev Rav, 3,* 24. [In Hebrew].

Farrell, W.C., Sapp, J.R., Johnson, M.J.H., & Pollard, D.S. (1994). Assessing college aspirations among at-risk high school students: A principle components analysis. *High School, 77,* 294–303.

Feige, M., & Shiloni, Z. (Eds.). (2008). *Archaeology and Nationalism in Eretz – Israel.* Ber Sheva: The Ben-Gurion Research Institute. [In Hebrew].

Fergus, E. (2009). Understanding Latino students' schooling experiences: The relevance of skin color among Mexican and Puerto Rican high school students. *Teachers College Record, 111*(2), 339–375.

Fisher, R.T. (1959). *Pattern for Soviet Youth: A Study of the Congress of the Komsomol, 1918–1954.* New York, NY: Columbia University.

Forum. (2002). Mizrachiut epistemology in Israel [In Hebrew]. In H. Hever, Y. Shenhav & P. Motzafi-Haller (Eds.) *Mizrahim in Israel: A Critical Observation into Israel's Ethnicity* (pp. 15–27). Jerusalem: Van Leer Institute. [In Hebrew].

Foundation for the Advancement of Egalitarian Academic Education in Israel (2019). Retrieved from https://kedma-edu.org.il. [In Hebrew].

Frankenstein, C. (1951). On the concept of primitivity. *Megamot, 2*(4), 339–360. [In Hebrew].

Frankenstein, C. (1952). The psychological approach to the problem of ethnic differences. *Megamot, 3*(3), 158–170. [In Hebrew].

Frankenstein, C. (1972a). *They Think Again: Summary of an Educational Experiment with Underprivileged Adolescents.* Jerusalem: The Hebrew University of Jerusalem. [In Hebrew].

Frankenstein, C. (1972b). *Unchaining Thinking: Rehabilitating the Intelligence of Underprivileged Youth – an Experiment and Its Analysis.* Jerusalem: The Hebrew University of Jerusalem. [In Hebrew].

Freire, P. (1962). *Pedagogy of the Oppressed.* New York, NY: Herder and Herder.

Freire, P. (1970). *Pedagogy of the Oppressed.* New York, NY: Continuum.

Freire, P. (1992). *Pedagogy of Hope.* New York, NY: Continuum.

Freire, P., & Shor, I. (1987). *A Pedagogy for Liberation: Dialogues on Transforming Education.* South Hadley, MA: Bergin and Garvey.

Gallagher, C., Hipkins, R., & Zohar, A. (2012). Positioning thinking within national curriculum and assessment system: Perspectives from Israel, New Zealand and Northern Ireland. *Thinking Skills and Creativity, 7*(2), 134–143.

Gamoran, A. (2001). American schooling and educational inequality: A forecast for the 21st century. *Sociology of Education, 74*(2), 135–153.

Geertz, C. (1973). *The Interpretation of Cultures.* New York, NY: Basic Books, Inc., Publishers.

Gellner, E. (1964). *Thought and Change.* Chicago, IL: University of Chicago Press.

Gellner, E. (1983). *Nations and Nationalism.* Oxford: Blackwell Publishing.

Gertel, G. (2002). *School Field Trips and their Significance for Educators and Students During the Period 1920–1980* (Doctoral dissertation). Tel Aviv University, Tel Aviv. [In Hebrew].

Getz (Gal), P. (2003). Sami Shalom Chetrit. In N. Baram (Ed.) *Masters of Culture, Anatomy of Israeli Culture Producers* (pp. 175–190). Tel Aviv: Am Oved Publishers. [In Hebrew].

Giroux, H. (2011). *On Critical Pedagogy*. New York, NY: Continuum.

Gispan, Y. (2009). *When the heart cries*. Retrieved from https://shironet.mako. co.il/artist?type=lyrics&lang=1&prfid=498&wrkid=1787 [In Hebrew].

Grebelsky-Lichtman, T., Bar Shalom, Y., & Bar Shalom, A. (2015). Dilemmas in school counselling: The case of two Jerusalem schools. *International Journal of Learner Diversity and Identities, 22*(4), 17–22.

Greenfeld, L. (1992). *Nationalism: Five Roads to Modernity*. Cambridge, MA: Harvard University Press.

Haberfeld, Y., & Cohen, Y. (1995). *Schooling and Income Gaps between Western and Eastern Jews in Israel, 1975–1992*. Discussion paper No. 80. Tel Aviv: Golda Meir Institute for Social and Labor Research. [In Hebrew].

Haberfeld, Y., & Cohen, Y. (2007). Gender, ethnic and national earnings gaps in Israel: The role of rising inequality. *Social Science Research, 36*(2), 654–672.

Hall, S. (2000). Old and new identities, old and new ethnicities. In J. Solmons & L. Back (Eds.) *Theories of Race and Racism: A Reader* (pp. 41–68). London and New York, NY: Routledge.

Hannum, E., & Buchmann, C. (2003). Global education expansion and socio-economic development: An assessment of findings from the social sciences. In J.E. Cohen, D.E. Bloom & M.B. Malin (Eds.) *Educating All Children: A Global Agenda*. Cambridge: MIT Press.

Hanson, S.L. (1994). Lost talent: Unrealized educational aspirations and expectations among U.S. youths. *Sociology of Education, 67*(3), 159–183.

Haramati, S. (2000). *The Pioneer Teachers in Eretz Israel*. Tel Aviv: Ministry of Defense. [In Hebrew].

Haski-Leventhal, D., Yogev-Keren, H., & Katz, H. (2011). *Philanthropy in Israel 2008: Pattern of Giving, Volunteering and Organ Donation of the Israeli Public*. Beer Sheva: The Israeli Center for Third Sector Research. [In Hebrew].

Herzog, H. (1987). Political ethnicity as a socially constructed reality: The case of Jews in Israel. In M.J. Esman & I. Rabinovitch (Eds.) *Ethnicity Pluralism and the State in the Middle East* (pp. 140–151). Ithaca, NY: Cornell University Press.

Hobsbawm, E. (1983). Mass-production traditions: Europe, 1870–1914. In E. Hobsbawm & T. Ranger (Eds.) *The Invention of Tradition* (pp. 263–308). New York, NY: Cambridge University Press.

hooks, b. (1994). *Engaged Pedagogy, Teaching to Transgress: Education as the Practice of Freedom*. London and New York, NY: Routledge.

Horowitz, A. (1999). Israeli Mediterranean music straddling disputed territories. *Journal of American Folklore, 112*(445), 450–463.

Ichilov, O. (2004). *Political Learning and Citizenship Education Under Conflict. The Political Socialization of Israeli and Palestinian Youngsters.* London and New York, NY: Routledge.

Jabareen, T.Y., & Agbaria, A. (2017). Minority educational autonomy rights: The case of Arab-Palestinians in Israel. *Virginia Journal of Social Policy & The Law, 24*(1), 26–55.

Jamal, A. (2007). Nationalizing states and the constitution of hollow citizenship: Israel and its Palestinian citizens. *Ethnopolitics, 6*(4), 471–493.

Kahane, R. (2007). *Youth and the Code of Informality.* Jerusalem: Bialik Institute. [In Hebrew].

Kahanoff, J. (1958). Reflections of a levantine Jew. *Jewish Frontier,* (April), 7–11.

Kao, G., & Tienda, M. (1995). Optimism and achievement: The educational performance of immigrant youth. *Social Science Quarterly, 76*(1), 1–19.

Kaplan, D. (2009). The songs of the siren: Engineering national time on Israeli radio. *Cultural Anthropology, 42*(2), 313–345.

Karpel, D. (2014). Why did the Mizrahi educational achievement fail? 20 years to Kedma. *Haaretz,* 19.7.2014. Retrieved from https://www.haaretz.co.il/magazine/.premium-1.2379015 [In Hebrew].

Katriel, T. (1994). Sites of memory: Discourse of the past in Israeli pioneering settlement museums. *Quarterly Journal of Speech, 80*(1), 1–20.

Kedma. (n.d). *Kedma – An Academic High School in the Community.* Jerusalem: Self publication. [In Hebrew].

Kedma. (1999). *Association of Friends of the Kedma School.* Jerusalem: Self publication. [In Hebrew].

Kedma. (2001). *Association of Friends of the Kedma School.* Jerusalem: Self publication. [In Hebrew].

Khattab, N. (2015). Students' aspiration, expectation and school achievement: What really matters? *British Educational Research Journal, 41*(5), 731–748.

Khazzoom, A. (2003). The great chain of orientalism: Jewish identity, stigma management and ethnic exclusion in Israel. *American Sociological Review, 68*(4), 481–511.

Khazzoom, A. (2008). *Shifting Ethnic Boundaries and inequality in Israel: Or, How the Polish Peddler Became a German Intellectual.* Stanford: Stanford University Press.

Kimmerling, B. (1993). Patterns of militarism in Israel. *European Journal of Sociology, 34*(2), 196–223.

Kimmerling, B. (2001). *The Invention and Decline of Israeliness: State, Society and the Military.* California: University of California Press.

Kohn, H. (1944). *The Idea of Nationalism: A Study in Its Origins and Background.* New York, NY: Collier Books.

Koopmans, R., & Statham, P. (1999). Challenging the liberal-nation state? Postnationalism, multiculturalism, and the collective claims making of migrants and ethnic minorities in Britain and Germany. *American Journal of Sociology, 105*(3), 652–696.

Kozłowska, M. (2014). Who am I? Mizrahi discourse on identity in contemporary Israel. *Hemispheres; Wroclaw, 29*(1), 47–61.

Lefebvre's, H. (1991). *The Production of Space*. Oxford: Blackwell.

Levy, G., & Sasson-Levy, O. (2008). Militarized socialization, military service and class reproduction: The experience of Israeli soldiers. *Sociological Perspectives*, *51*(2), 349–374.

Levy, L. (2017). The Arab Jew debates: Media, culture, politics, history. *Journal of Levantine Studies*, *17*(1), 79–103.

Levy, Y. (2006). The war of the Peripheries: A social mapping of the IDF casualties in the Al-Aqsa Intifada. *Social Identities*, *12*(3), 309–324.

Levy, Y., Lomsky-Feder, E., & Harel, N. (2007). From 'obligatory militarism' to 'contractual militarism': Competing models of citizenship. *Israel Studies*, *12*(1), 48–127.

Lobman, C. (2011). Democracy and development: The role of outside-of-school experiences in preparing young people to be active citizens. *Democracy & Education*, *19*(1), 1–9.

Lomsky-Feder, E. (2004). The memorial ceremony in Israeli schools: Between the states and civil society. *British Journal of Sociology of Education*, *25*(3), 291–305.

Lomsky-Feder, E., & Ben Ari, E. (1999). From 'the people in uniform' to 'different uniforms for the people': Professionalism, diversity and the Israeli defense forces. In J. Soeters & J. van der Meulen (Eds.) *Managing Diversity in Armed Forces: Experiences from Nine Countries* (pp. 157–186). Tilburg: Tilburg University Press.

Lucas, S.R., & Berends, M. (2002). Sociodemographic diversity, correlated achievement, and de facto tracking. *Sociology of Education*, *75*(4), 328–348.

Lustick, I. (1999). Israel as a non-Arab state: The political implication of mass immigration of non-Jews. *Middle East Journal*, *53*(3), 417–433.

Lutkus, A., & Weiss, A. (2007). *The Nation's Report Card: Civics 2006*. Washington, DC: National Center for Education Statistics.

Lutz, C. (2002). Making war at home in the United States: Militarization and the current crisis. *American Anthropologist*, *104*(3), 723–735.

Margolin, Y. (1947). *The Path to Nature*. Merhavia: Hakibbutz Haartzy. [In Hebrew].

Markovich, Y.D. (1999). *Local and Universal Aspects in the Curriculum of Specialty Schools: The Case of Kedma School in the Tiqva Neighborhood of South Tel Aviv* (Master's thesis). The Hebrew University of Jerusalem, Jerusalem. [In Hebrew].

Markovich, Y.D. (2012). Who owns education for peace and for war? Peace/war industry and ethnic stratification: The case of one underprivileged school in Israel. In P.R. Carr & B.J. Porfilio (Eds.) *Education for Peace in a Time of Permanent War: Are Schools Part of the Solution or the Problem?* (pp. 183–196). New York, London: Routledge.

Markovich, Y.D. (2013a). Lessons learned from a study of a Jewish Israeli high school: Critical pedagogy in contention. *InterActions, UCLA Journal of Education and Information Studies*, *9*(2), 1–18.

Markovich, Y.D., & Rapoport, T. (2013b). Creating art, creating identity: Under-privileged pupils in art education challenge critical pedagogy practices. *International Journal of Education through Art*, *9*(1), 7–22.

Markovich, Y.D. (2014). Grades are not enough: Critical pedagogy, achievements and the self-perception of successful underprivileged pupils. *Global Educational Research Journal, 2*(8), 141–151.

Markovich, Y.D. (2016). Ethnicity vs. nationality in one nationalized educational site. *Critical Studies in Education, 57*(2), 238–253.

McLaren, P., & Kincheloe, J.L. (2007). *Critical Pedagogy: Where are We Now?* New York, NY: Peter Lang.

Menachem, N. (1983). *Ethnic Tensions and Discrimination in Israel: Socio-Historical Aspects.* Ramat Gan: Rubin Press. [In Hebrew].

Menashe, H. (2015). *When Something looks Crooked, Straighten it Up.* Kedma Association: Jerusalem.

Mickelson, R.A. (2001). Subverting swann: First- and second-generation segregation in the Charlotte-Mecklenburg schools. *American Educational Research Journal, 38*(2), 215–252.

Mishory, A. (1990). Is the Bauhaus needed? – The main thing is succeeding in the matriculation exams. *Studio, 16*, 16–17. [In Hebrew].

Mitchell, W.J.T. (Ed.). (1994). *Landscapes and Power.* Chicago, IL: The Chicago University Press.

Mizrachi, N. (2004). 'From badness to sickness': The role of ethnopsychology in shaping ethnic hierarchies in Israel. *Social identities, 10*(2), 219–243.

Mizrachi, N., Goodman, Y.C., & Feniger, Y. (2009) 'I don't want to see it': decoupling ethnicity and class from social structure in Jewish Israeli high schools. *Ethnic and Racial Studies, 32*(7), 1203–1225.

Mizrachi, N., & Herzog, H. (2012). Participatory Destigmatization strategies among Palestinian citizens of Israel, Ethiopian Jews and Mizrahi Jews. *Ethnic and Racial Studies, 35*(3), 418–435.

Muller, C., Riegle-Crumb, C., Schiller, K.S., Wilkinson, L., & Frank, K.A. (2010). Race and academic achievement in racially diverse high schools: Opportunity and stratification. *Teachers College Record, 112*(4), 1038–1063.

Narkis, L. (2011). *Mama's soldier.* Retrieved from https://shironet.mako.co.il/artist?type=lyrics&lang=1&prfid=594&wrkid=8924 [In Hebrew].

Ogbu, J.U. (1978). *Minority Education and Caste.* New York, NY: Academic Press.

Ogbu, J.U. (1990). Minority education in comparative perspective. *The Journal Negro Education, 59*(1), 45–57.

Ogbu, J.U. (1991). Low Performance as an adaptation: The case of blacks in Stockton, California. In M.A. Gibson & J.U. Ogbu (Eds.) *Minority Status Schooling* (pp. 249–285). New York, NY: Garland.

Ohana, D. (2011). *Israel and Its Mediterranean Identity.* New York: Palgrave Macmillan.

Ofrat, G. (1987). The myth of creativity. In H. Unger (Ed.) *Art as an Educational Challenge: A Collection for the 40th Anniversary of the Midrasha* (pp. 45–53). kfar Saba: Beit Berl College. [In Hebrew].

Orian, D. (2001). Teaching the performing arts: Ideological aspects. *Bamah, 164*, 54–69. [In Hebrew].

Pearson, D. (1988). From communality to ethnicity: Some theoretical considerations on the Maori ethnic revival. *Ethnic and Racial Studies, 11*(2), 168–191.

Peled, Y. (2008). The evolution of Israeli citizenship: An overview. *Citizenship Studies, 12*(3), 335–345.

Piterberg, G. (1996). Domestic orientalism: The representation of 'oriental' Jews in Zionist/Israeli historiography. *British Journal of Middle Eastern Studies, 23*(2), 125–145.

Podeh, E. (2000). History and memory in the Israeli education system. *History and Memory, 12*(spring), 65–100.

Poltin, S. (2009). The annual school trip and boundaries of responsibility, or: Where were the teachers? *Café the Marker,* 1.1.2009. Retrieved from http://cafe.themarker.com/view.php?t=1337946 [In Hebrew].

Portes, A., & MacLeod, D. (1996). Educational progress of children of immigrants: The roles of class, ethnicity and school context. *Sociology of Education, 69*(4), 255–275.

Rabinowitz, D. (2001). The Palestinian citizens of Israel, the concept of trapped minority and the discourse of transnationalism in anthropology. *Ethnic and Racial Studies, 24*(1), 64–85.

Ram, U. (2000). National, ethnic or civic? Contesting paradigms of memory, identity and culture in Israel. *Studies in Philosophy and Education, 19*(5–6), 405–422.

Ramey, C.T., & Suarez, T.M. (1985). Early intervention and the early experience paradigm: Toward a better framework of social policy. *Journal of Children in Contemporary Society, 7*(1), 1–13.

Raz-Krakotzkin, A. (2013). Exile, history, and the nationalization of Jewish memory: Some reflections on the Zionist notion of history and return. *Journal of Levantine Studies, 3*(2), 37–70.

Regev, M. (2000). To have a culture of our own: On Israeliness and its variants. *Ethnic and Racial Studies, 23*(2), 223–247.

Renan. E. [1882] (1990). What is a nation? In H.K. Bhabha (Ed.) *Nation and Narration* (pp. 8–22). London and New York, NY: Routledge.

Resnik, J. (2006). Alternative identities in multicultural schools in Israel: Emancipatory identity, mixed identity and transnational identity. *British Journal of Sociology of Education, 27*(5), 585–601.

Riger, E. (1945). *The Vocational Education in the Jewish Society in the Land of Israel.* Jerusalem: The Hebrew University of Jerusalem. [In Hebrew].

Rigsby, L.C., Stull, J.C., & Morse-Kelley, J. (1997). Determinants of student educational expectations and achievement: Race and gender differences. In R.D. Taylor & M.C. Wang (Eds.) *Social and Emotional Adjustment and Family Relations in Ethnic Minority Families* (pp. 201–224). Mahwah, NJ: Erlbaum.

Roeh, Y. (1989). *The fruits from your garden.* Retrieved from https://shironet.mako.co.il/artist?type=lyrics&lang=1&prfid=488&wrkid=2659 [In Hebrew].

Roginsky, D. (2009). The national, ethnic and the between: A sociological examination of the relationship between folkdance, ethnic dance and dance of minorities in Israel. In H. Rottenberg & D. Roginsky (Eds.) *Dance Discourse in Israel* (pp. 95–125). Tel Aviv: Resling. [In Hebrew].

Rohde, A. (2012). Bridging conflicts through history education? A case study from Israel/Palestine. In A. Samira, R. Achim & D. Sarhan (Eds.) *The Politics of Educational Reform in the Middle-East, Self and Other in Textbooks and Curricula* (pp. 237–260). New York, NY and Oxford: Berghahn Books.

Ronen, D. (1999). Art education in Israel. In E. Peled (Ed.) *Fifty Years of Israeli Education* (pp. 717–742). Jerusalem: Israeli Ministry of Education, Culture and Sports. [In Hebrew].

Rubowitz, M. (2007). "Individual commitment" as a non-formal educational program. In S. Romi & M. Schmida (Eds.) *Non-Formal Education in a Changing Reality* (pp. 399–409). Jerusalem: The Magnes Press. [In Hebrew].

Saada-Ophir, G. (2006). Borderland pop: Arab-Jewish musicians and the politics of performance. *Cultural Anthropology, 21*(2), 205–233.

Sabar, Y. (1989). Studies of the folklore, ethnography and literature of Kurdistani Jews: An annotated bibliography. *Jewish Folklore and Ethnology Review, II*(1–2), 35–38.

Saporta, I., & Yonah, Y. (2004). Pre-vocational education: The making of Israel's ethno-working class. *Race, Ethnicity and Education, 7*(3), 251–275.

Sasson-Levi, O., & Shoshana, A. (2013). "Passing" as (non)ethnic: The Israeli version of acting white. *Sociological Inquiry, 83*(3), 4448–4472.

Sasson-Levy, O. (2002). Constructing identities at the margins: Masculinities and citizenship in the Israeli army. *Sociological Quarterly, 43*(2), 357–383.

Schama, S. (1995). *Landscape and Memory.* New York, NY: Vintage Books.

Semyonov, M., & Lewin-Epstein, N. (Eds.). (2004). *Stratification in Israel: Class, Ethnicity and Gender.* London: Transaction.

Shachar, Y.I. (2013). White management of 'volunteering': Ethnographic evidence from an Israeli NGO. *VOLUNTAS: International Journal of Voluntary and Nonprofit Organizations, 25*(6), 1417–1440.

Shafir, G., & Peled, Y. (2002). *Being Israeli: The Dynamics of Multiple Citizenship.* New York, NY: Cambridge University Press.

Shapira, A. (1997). *New Jews Old Jews.* Tel Aviv: Am Oved. [In Hebrew].

Shapira, A. (2005). *The Bible and Israeli Identity.* Jerusalem: The Hebrew University. [In Hebrew].

Sharaby, R. (2011). Political activism and ethnic revival of a cultural symbol. *Ethnicities, 11*(4), 489–511.

Shemer, N. (1966). *We're from the same village.* Retrieved from https://shironet.mako.co.il/artist?type=lyrics&lang=1&prfid=738&wrkid=4356 [In Hebrew].

Shemer, N. (1973). *All we pray for.* Retrieved from https://shironet.mako.co.il/artist?type=lyrics&lang=1&prfid=738&wrkid=1895 [In Hebrew].

Shemer, N. (1979). *The middle of Tammuz.* Retrieved from https://shironet.mako.co.il/artist?type=lyrics&lang=1&prfid=738&wrkid=2576 [In Hebrew].

Shemer, Y. (2007). Victimhood, protest, and agency in contemporary Mizrahi (Arab-Jewish) films in Israel. *Scope, 8*, 1–27.

Shenhav, Y. (2006). *The Arab Jews: A Postcolonial Reading of Nationalism, Religion, and Ethnicity.* Stanford: Stanford University Press.

Shenhav, Y., & Hever, H. (2012). Arab Jews after structuralism: Zionist discourse and the (de)formation of an ethnic identity. *Social Identities, 18*(1), 99–116.Shohat, E. (1999). The invention of the Mizrahim. *Journal of Palestine Studies, 29*(1), 5–20.

Shor, I. (1992). *Empowering Education: Critical Teaching for Social Change.* Chicago, IL: University of Chicago Press.

Shoshana, A. (2017). Ethnographies of 'a lesson in racism': Class, ethnicity, and the supremacy of the psychological discourse. *Anthropology & Education Quarterly, 48*(1), 61–76.

Smilansky, M., & Nevo, D. (1979). *The Gifted Disadvantaged: A Ten-Year Longitudinal Study of Compensatory Education in Israel.* London: Gordon and Breach.

Smith, D.A. (1986). *The Ethnic Origins of Nations.* Oxford: Blackwell Publishers.

Smith D.A. (2009). *Ethno-Symbolism and Nationalism – A Cultural Approach.* London and New York, NY: Routledge.

Spektorowski, A. (2000). The French new right: Differentialism and the idea of Ethnophilian exclusionism. *Polity, 33*(2), 283–304.

Springhall, J. (1977). *Youth, Empire and Society, British Youth Movements, 1883–1940.* London: Croom Helm.

Stadler, N., Lomsky-Feder, E., & Ben-Ari, E. (2008). Fundamentalism's encounters with citizenship: The Haredim in Israel. *Citizenship Studies, 12*(3), 215–231.

State Comptroller. (1996). *The Annual School Trip* (47), 20–42. Jerusalem: State Comptroller. [In Hebrew].

Steele, C.M., Spencer, S.J., & Aronson, J. (2002). Contending with group image: The psychology of stereotype and social identity threat. *Advances in Experimental Social Psychology, 34*, 379–440.

Steinhardt, M. (2004). *Trends in the Teaching of Drawing in Hebrew Schools in the "Yishuv" Pre-State period and in Israel, 1906–1996, as Reflected in School Curicula'* (Doctoral dissertation). Tel Aviv University, Tel Aviv. [In Hebrew].

Swirski, S. (1999). *Politics and Education in Israel.* New York, NY: Falmer Press.

Swirski, S., & Atkin, A. (2002). *Entitlement to Matriculation Certificates According to Settlements 2000–2001.* Tel Aviv: Adva Center for Research of the Society in Israel. [In Hebrew].

Swirski, S., & Dagan-Buzaglo, N. (2009). *Separation, Inequality and Faltering Leadership, Education in Israel.* Tel Aviv: Adva Center. [In Hebrew].

Swirski, S., & Dagan-Buzaglo, N. (2011). *Education Reform: Making Education Work for all Children.* Tel Aviv: Adva Center. [In Hebrew].

Swirski, S., Konor-Atias, E., & Dagan-Buzaglo, N. (2016). Where is the other half of the age cohort? Twelfth graders who don't matriculate. *Adva Center, Information on equality and Social Justice in Israel.* Retrieved from https://adva.org/en/education2016-17/

Tabib-Calif, Y. (2015). *Ethnicity on the Move: Boundary Work and Life Trajectories of Young Adults* (Doctoral dissertation). The Hebrew University of Jerusalem, Jerusalem. [In Hebrew].

Tabib-Calif, Y., & Lomsky-Feder, E. (2014). Symbolic boundary work in schools: Demarcating and denying ethnic boundaries. *Anthropology and Education, 45*(1), 22–38.

Tilly, C. (1996). The emergence of citizenship in France and elsewhere. *International Review of Social History, 40*(3), 223–236.

Tomlinson, S. (1982). *Sociology of Special Education*. London and New York, NY: Routledge and Kegan Paul.

Toren, Z. (2007). Attitude towards artwork in the Israeli kindergarten and the reproduction of social status. *Studies in Art Education, 48*(2), 172–188.

van den Berghe, P. (1978). Race and ethnicity: A sociobiological perspective. *Ethnic and Racial Studies, 1*(4), 401–411.

Vardi, M., Orr, Z., & Finkelstein, A. (2019). Civic engagement of students from minority groups: The case of ultra-orthodox students and communities in Jerusalem. In D.Y. Markovich, D. Golan & N. Shalhoub-Kevorkian (Eds.) *Engaged Students in Conflict Zones, Community-Engaged Courses in Israel as a Vehicle for Change* (pp. 261–292). London: Palgrave Macmillan Press.

Weber, E. (2003). The myth of the nation and the creation of the "Other". *Critical Review, 15*(3–4), 387–402.

Weiss, M. (1997). Bereavement, commemoration, and collective identity in contemporary Israeli society. *Anthropological Quarterly, 70*(2), 91–100.

Westheimer, J. (Ed.). (2007). *Pledging Alliances: The Politics of Patriotism in America's Schools*. New York, NY: Teachers College Press.

Yacobi, H. (2008). Architecture, orientalism, and identity: The politics of the Israeli-built emolument. *Israel Studies, 13*(1), 94–118.

Yaish, M. (2001). Class structure in a deeply divided society: Class and ethnic inequality in Israel 1074–1991. *The British Journal of Sociology, 52*(3), 409–437.

Yehoshua, Y. (2017). IDF notes drop in motivation to serve in combat roles. *Y Net*, 16.8.17. Retrieved from https://www.ynetnews.com/articles/0,7340, L-5003535,00.html

Yemini, M., Bar-Nissan, H., & Shavit, Y. (2014). Cosmopolitanism versus nationalism in Israeli education. *Comparative Education Review, 58*(4), 708–728.

Yifatchel, O. (1998). The internal frontier: Territorial control and ethnic relations in Israel. In O. Yiftachel & A. Meir (Eds.) *Ethnic Frontiers and Peripheries: Landscapes of Development and Inequality in Israel* (pp. 39–68). Boulder, CO: Westview Press.

Yona, I. (2002). *Voices from the Katamonim Neighborhood*. Tel Aviv: Andalus. [In Hebrew].

Yona, I., & Zalmanson Levi, G. (2004). This and that, the curricula at Kedma School. In D. Golan-Agnon (Ed.) *Inequality in Education* (pp. 188–208). Tel Aviv: Babel. [In Hebrew].

Yonah, Y., Dahan, Y., & Markovich, Y.D. (2008). Neo-liberal reforms in Israel's education system: The dialectics of the state. *International Studies in Sociology of Education*, *18*(3–4), 199–217.

Yonah, Y., Na'aman, Y., & Machlev, D. (Eds.). (2007). *Rainbow of Opinions, A Mizrahi Agenda to the Israeli Society*. Tel Aviv: November Books. [In Hebrew].

Yonah, Y., Ram, H., & Markovich, Y.D. (2010). Family structure. *Cultural Dynamics*, *22*(3), 197–223.

Zelda. (1974). *Each of us has a name*. Retrieved from https://shironet.mako.co.il/artist?type=lyrics&lang=1&prfid=383&wrkid=1964 [In Hebrew].

Zerubavel, Y. (1995). *Recovered Roots: Collective Memory and the Making of Israeli National Tradition*. Chicago, IL: The University of Chicago Press.

Zirkel, S. (2008). The influence of multicultural educational practices on student outcomes and intergroup relations. *Teachers College Records*, *110*(6), 1147–1181.

Zmora Cohen, M. (1985). *The Report of Art Education – The Pedagogical Bureau*. Jerusalem: Israeli Ministry of Education, Culture and Sports. [In Hebrew].

Index

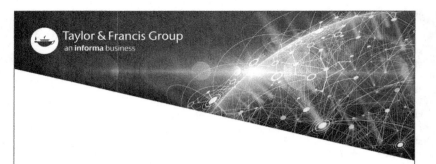

Printed in the United States
by Baker & Taylor Publisher Services